YOU CAN

Have a CREATIVE classroom

Sue Cowl[ey]

The best-selling a[uthor]
of *Getting the Bugg[ers to]*
Behave and *You Ca[n Have]*
a Calm Classroom

FOR AGE[S]

7-1[1]

"When individu[als]
strengths, it ca[n]
[im]pact on self-esteem and achie[ve]
National Advisory Committee on Creative and Cultura[l]

Acknowledgements

Author
Sue Cowley

Editor
Kathleen McCully

Development Editor
Kate Pedlar

Project Editor
Fabia Lewis

Series Designer
Catherine Perera

Cover Designers
Andrea Lewis/ Anna Oliwa

Cover photography
© Corbis/Punchstock

Design and Illustrations
Q2a Media

Text © Sue Cowley
© 2008 Scholastic Ltd
Designed using Adobe InDesign

Published by Scholastic Ltd
Villiers House
Clarendon Avenue
Leamington Spa
Warwickshire CV32 5PR

www.scholastic.co.uk

Printed by Bell and Bain Ltd
1 2 3 4 5 6 7 8 9   8 9 0 1 2 3 4 5 6 7

The publishers gratefully acknowledge:

Woodlands Junior School Kent, Lever Fabergé Ltd for Dove's Campaign For Real Beauty and Edward de Bono for permission to reference their websites.

British Library Cataloguing-in-Publication Data
A catalogue record for this book is available from the British Library.

ISBN 978-0439-94535-6

The right of Sue Cowley to be identified as the author of this work has been asserted by her in accordance with the Copyright, Designs and Patents Act 1988.

© Crown copyright and other Crown copyright material. Reproduced under the terms of the Click Use Licence.

Due to the nature of the web, the publisher cannot guarantee the content or links of any of the websites referred to. It is the responsibility of the reader to assess the suitability of websites. All websites in this book were accessed in July 2007.

Every effort has been made to trace copyright holders for the works reproduced in this book, and the publishers apologise for any inadvertent omissions.

Contents

Contents

Introduction

One of the real joys of being a teacher is getting involved in the more creative aspects of the job. Of course, planning for and teaching subjects such as art, dance, drama and music will require you to use your imaginative talents. But creativity also has a place in the way that you teach all curriculum areas, including those outside the arts disciplines.

As well as teaching different subjects in a creative way, you can also apply lots of imagination and creativity to the way that you manage your classroom and your pupils. You might be organising a beautiful display, trying out some new rewards, or experimenting with different ways of setting out your classroom. Through all of these things, and many more, creativity can become a natural and normal part of your everyday professional life.

Ideas about the 'best' way of teaching come and go. At times, the focus is on skills and discrete subjects; at other times, the idea of teaching in a multi-disciplinary way will be at the fore. Thankfully, we are currently going through a time when 'creativity' is viewed as vital – and it has become synonymous with teaching in an innovative and interesting way.

Children of all ages and abilities respond really well to getting involved in creative activities, and also to being taught in a creative way. From the earliest age, they will experiment with a simple object, such as a cardboard box, putting their imagination to the test to see what the box might become. Even the youngest children love to get involved in role playing; the classic 'mums and dads' or 'doctors and nurses' helps them gain an insight into relationships, situations and people.

Creativity is not only fun and key to good teaching; it can also be the solution to some of the difficulties we face in the classroom. Where behaviour is a problem, and all the usual strategies have failed, it is often the most bizarre or imaginative idea that suddenly helps you connect with a child.

In this book, you will find lots of ideas for approaches and activities to help make your classroom a more creative place. These ideas are practical, realistic, fun and reasonably easy to use. Hopefully, this book will inspire you to take a few risks with your teaching, to experiment and to incorporate creativity into your classroom as often as possible.

You Can... Get creative with your body

There are many similarities between teachers and actors. One of the key areas of likeness is that we both use our bodies to communicate with an audience. The more expressive and inventive we can be in doing this, the more effective our communication will be.

Thinking points

● Teachers communicate a great deal without even opening their mouths. What your body 'says' both consciously and subconsciously can have a big influence on how your pupils behave and work.

● Getting creative with your body is often a case of thinking 'outside the box'. Learn to analyse the way that you usually move around the room, and then do something completely different to give your pupils a surprise.

● Your hands are a particularly expressive part of your body. Aim to communicate lots of routine information with them – for instance, indicating that you want the children to stand up by lifting your hands with palms upwards.

Tips, ideas and activities

● Find creative ways of using your body to indicate when you need the class's attention. If you are confident enough to use more unusual methods, you will find that the more bizarre an approach is, the better it will work. For instance, you could:
  ● suddenly remove your eyes from the class and stare at the ceiling – because we normally give our pupils plenty of eye contact, this is a simple way of saying 'I'm waiting';
  ● clap out, click or tap a rhythmic pattern on a desk;
  ● 'freeze' your face and body completely still and hold this position until the class stops to see what on earth you are doing;
  ● strike a weird pose or do a dance in the style of *Saturday Night Fever*;
  ● hide behind your desk – hopefully the children will come and find you!

● Experiment with all the different shapes and patterns you can make around the classroom using your body. You might:
  ● circle the classroom to 'visit' all the children – your instinct will probably take you in a clockwise direction; try going anticlockwise as well;
  ● weave in and out of the desks;
  ● try taking a diagonal route across the room;
  ● think up and down as well as around – stand on a chair to make a point, or crouch down beside a child to talk about the work.

● Change the way that your body appears, by putting on an unusual outfit and role playing a different character. You could:
  ● wear a white lab coat to play the part of a 'government scientist';
  ● put on a police helmet to kick-start some investigation work;
  ● dress up as a character in a book, and get the children to hot-seat you to find out more about you.

You Can... Get creative with your voice

Your voice is a key part of what makes you a good teacher. The more interesting and stimulating the sound of your voice is, the better your pupils will listen to and understand what you say. You can have great fun getting creative with what you say and the way that you say it.

Thinking points

● Our children spend a big part of each day listening to us talk. If our vocal sound is interesting and engaging, rather than flat and dull, this will inevitably help the children connect with what we are saying.

● It is all too easy to get into bad vocal habits. Learn to listen to yourself as you talk, adapting your voice as you go along. Ask too for some feedback from the children about their perspective on the way that you sound.

● Teachers do need to take great care of their voices – we only have the one, after all. Aim to speak as little as possible – you can communicate a great deal without actually opening your mouth.

Tips, ideas and activities

● Add tone to your voice to create interest and increase your pupils' engagement with what you are saying. You could use:
  ● an excited tone to give the sense that the work is going to be fun;
  ● a sad or disappointed tone if the children are misbehaving;
  ● a scary tone to tell a spooky story.

● Vary the pace of your voice to add interest to your teaching. You might:
  ● speak quickly to energise and excite the class;
  ● use a sharp, staccato sound to make a point;
  ● stretch out the length of certain words to emphasise them (imagine you are stretching the word like a piece of chewing gum).

● If you are brave enough, try playing around with some different accents, dialects or languages. You might:
  ● take the register in another language, so that you and your pupils learn to say 'good morning' in languages from around the world, for instance: 'bom dia' (Portuguese) or 'guten morgen' (German);
  ● incorporate phrases from different dialects in your teaching, particularly if you are originally from another region;
  ● ask your pupils to teach you a few slang phrases and use these in a jokey way in your classroom;
  ● make up a few new words, creating a classroom language of your own.

● Experiment with different volumes to see the effect that this has on your pupils. Try whispering some instructions to get the children to listen more carefully, or using a megaphone or microphone to address the class.

● Experiment with different vocal sounds as well. You might:
  ● sing;
  ● roar;
  ● click your tongue;
  ● whistle;
  ● laugh!

You Can... **Use creative reward systems**

The rewards that teachers devise are often a highly creative part of their classroom management systems. This is particularly true at primary level, where the kind of rewards used are often amazingly diverse. Thinking of ways to make your reward systems more creative can be a very enjoyable part of the job.

Thinking points

● Schools will often put a set of rewards in place and keep them the same for a long time. Rewards do tend to go 'stale' after a while, and it is worth refreshing your system regularly.

● A reward will often stand for something else – it is a marker of the fact that the teacher approves, is pleased or has taken time to notice good effort, work or behaviour.

● Some children will work hard and behave well without the need for extrinsic rewards; others will need almost constant approval in order to keep going. Of course, this depends a great deal on the pupil's background.

● It is worth taking care over how you give rewards – do not always use them as a way of keeping tricky children in line. Remind yourself to praise the hard-working pupils as well.

Tips, ideas and activities

● Try making a whole-class reward system which incorporates an interesting display. This offers a good way of engaging and inspiring your pupils. Here are some suggestions:
  ● Draw a large animal picture to go on the wall (for example, a caterpillar) – as the children do well, they get to colour in sections of the picture. When the picture is completed, the whole class gets a reward.
  ● Make a sky/weather picture and create shapes to stick on: a sun, some clouds, rain, lightning and a rainbow. Use the shapes to indicate how pleased/unhappy you are with the class (keep the rainbow for when you are delighted!).

● Many schools are now sending postcards home as part of their reward system. This kind of home/school contact is a great idea, and is very motivational for the children. Here are a couple of useful tips about making the most of this approach:
  ● Get the children to design their own postcard, then choose a winning design (or several designs) and reproduce them. This helps give the children ownership of the system.
  ● At the start of the year, hand out a postcard to each of the children and ask them to fill in their parents' names and addresses. Put the postcards in your drawer, ready to use as appropriate. Again, this helps involve the children in the system, and means they know that you are ready to fill out a postcard and send it off at any time.

  ● Have a 'star of the week' award – the child who wins gets to sit on a special 'throne' for the day, wear a crown and be presented with a trophy.

You Can... Model creativity for your children

If we are asking our children to be more creative, it is only right that we are brave enough to take creative chances ourselves. By modelling imaginative activities for your pupils, you will show them that everyone and anyone can be creative (adults as well as children!).

Thinking points

- With any creative venture, there is an element of risk involved for you when you share your creativity with your class. Putting ourselves on the line, and allowing others to comment on what we produce, is a crucial part of any imaginative activity.

- By showing a willingness to take such risks, you will show your pupils that it is OK to express themselves creatively. Often, the process of being creative is more important and interesting than the judgements that others might make on what we have done.

- As well as the teacher modelling creativity for his or her class, it is also well worth trying to bring in some visitors who work in the creative fields. Ask around among parents, or explore the various residency projects (writers, artists) that take place around the UK.

Tips, ideas and activities

- When you are studying an area which involves creative thinking, vocalise the thought processes you are using as you introduce the topic. This will help your pupils learn how to use metacognition – the process by which we understand our own thinking. As you speak, use vocabulary which expresses what is going on inside your head. For example, you might use phrases such as:
  - *I was wondering how this…*
  - *I'm curious to find out…*
  - *I'm not sure what I think about…*
  - *I was asking myself how…*

- Share examples of your own creativity with your pupils, showing them that you are willing to participate in and model examples for the class. Allow the children to give feedback (both positive and negative) on the creative pieces you have done. This approach requires an element of bravery, which is after all what we ask from our children! You might share with them:
  - poems and stories that you wrote as a child, if you have any old exercise books from your school days;
  - an essay that you wrote while you were at university;
  - an artistic photograph that you have taken;
  - examples from a hobby that you enjoy, for instance, some pottery you have made, or some photos of your garden.

- Be creative in the ways that you teach; this will show your pupils how we can be personally creative in many areas of our lives. Your creative teaching style will include the ways that you use your voice, your body, space, and so on.

- Get creative with your appearance by wearing a costume for a history project or modelling some accessories to kick-start a design project.

You Can... Use experimental approaches to teaching

The idea that teachers can be experimental with their teaching has fallen out of favour over the last couple of decades. There have been so many curriculum changes, initiatives, tick boxes and risk assessments that we hardly dare do anything unusual. Thankfully, the pendulum finally seems to be swinging back in the other direction.

Thinking points

● It is tempting to avoid creative approaches, because of the pressure to get through the curriculum, and also perhaps because of fears about how the children will react to being given something unusual to do. This is a real shame – by taking a few risks with how you teach, and consequently giving the children your trust, you can achieve some really high quality, inspirational teaching and learning.

● It is possible to be experimental with how you teach in all different areas of the curriculum. And perhaps the most creative approach is to bring innovative, imaginative ideas into the more traditional, core subjects.

Tips, ideas and activities

● Try out some organic, open-ended lessons – ones where the children direct the learning, without a specific aim, objective, success criteria or similar in mind. If you are nervous about teaching without an 'end result', ask the children to devise an outcome for what they will achieve by the end of the lesson. You might:
- show an interesting object to the class and ask the children what they would like to find out about it;
- give the children a single word ('trust', 'morality') as a starting point for a philosophical discussion;
- begin a topic by asking the children to devise a list of questions they want answered.

● Drama is great for bringing experimental approaches into your teaching. If you are nervous about how your pupils might react to too much freedom, try some tightly structured exercises. This 'thought tunnel' activity can be adapted to lots of different subjects. Here is how it works:
- Find an open space – a hall or gym, or clear the furniture to the sides of your room.
- Get the children into pairs and ask them to make two straight lines, down the middle of the space, facing their partners, standing a person's width apart.
- Choose a focus for the activity; for instance, exploring forgiveness in a topic about Christian beliefs and actions.
- Ask for a volunteer to walk down the tunnel. Explain to the class that this person has done something wrong (for example, taken a toy without asking).
- As the volunteer passes, the other children voice their thoughts: *How dare you steal my toy?*; *That's a horrible thing to do!* Afterwards, talk about how the experience felt.
- Now repeat the activity, this time forgiving the person: *I forgive you for what you did; It's OK, I don't mind.* Again, discuss the experience.

You Can... Develop your children's creative thinking

As well as being an important skill in many school subjects, creative thinking can also help us a great deal in our day-to-day lives. It is particularly useful when we come up against a problem that needs solving, as it can help us to find original, often innovative solutions.

Thinking points

● Creative thinking is highly prized in our modern world, in many different disciplines. It is of course valuable in the arts subjects, but it also features in areas such as design, engineering, science and so on.

● This type of thought may also be about making something new, or finding a fresh approach to an old problem. Many of the ideas and inventions that we consider completely normal and natural (aeroplanes, the internet) first came about as a result of someone's creative thought.

● Teachers, and perhaps especially primary teachers, tend to be very creative thinkers. During a typical school day, you will come up against, and hopefully solve, a whole range of issues and problems. Often, the more creatively you do this, the better the results will be.

Tips, ideas and activities

● Use the classic 'ten uses for a' activity to brainstorm lots of creative ideas. This works best if you have actual examples of the objects to show the children. You could ask your pupils to come up ten uses for:
  ● a paperclip;
  ● an alarm clock;
  ● a piece of paper;
  ● a coconut.

● Set your pupils some practical problem-solving activities to encourage them to think creatively. Give them access to a range of resources to use in their quest to find creative solutions. Take away the option of using the most obvious solution, to force them into taking alternative routes. For instance, you might ask them to:
  ● move a cardboard box from one side of the room to the other, without touching it;
  ● work out how much sand they can fit in an empty jar, without actually filling it up;
  ● find out how much a rock weighs, without using scales;
  ● move a child who is standing on a skateboard, without touching them.

● Use a crime scene scenario to encourage creative thinking. Here is how it works:
  ● Set up a 'crime scene' in one corner of the room; for instance, a scene from a robbery or a murder.
  ● Use props to stage the crime, allowing the children to examine the evidence wearing plastic gloves.
  ● If possible, use crime scene tape to add realism (you can get this from various internet sites, such as www.uktapes.com).
  ● Ask the children to act as 'police detectives' to solve the crime, coming up with a theory about what happened.
  ● Ask them what they want to do next – for example, test for forensic evidence, interview witnesses and so on.
  ● Get the children to stage a reconstruction of the crime.

You Can... Use role play to develop creativity

Becoming someone or something else requires us to think and behave in a creative way. Although we can never fully know what it is like to be another person, the skills required to take on a character can help us understand how other people might think or feel.

Thinking points

● Although role play is used a great deal in the lower end of the primary age range, we may feel that we have less need (or less time available) to use it with children at Key Stage 2.

● Role play is often seen as something specific to drama or an English lesson. In fact, role play can offer a great way into many different subject areas, particularly for topic work in history, science and RE.

● By exploring and examining how different people or characters think, feel and behave, your children will learn how to develop empathy with others.

● They will also see how people behave differently in certain situations, times or contexts. This can help them learn how to adapt their own behaviour so that it is appropriate for a particular situation.

Tips, ideas and activities

● Use the drama technique called 'role of the expert' to approach factual-based work in a variety of subjects. To use this technique:

● Ask that the children work 'in role' as a person or character.

● Get them to take on the attributes, skills, experiences or approaches of that person.

● Give them a range of jobs, tasks or situations that this person might face. This could include problem solving, researching, group discussions, writing in role and so on.

● Here are some ideas for using the 'role of the expert' to approach some of the QCA schemes of work (see www. standards.dfes.gov.uk/schemes3).

● Science: during the unit on 'Keeping healthy', the children work in role as 'personal trainers' or 'dietary consultants' to devise programmes for people with a variety of needs, fitness levels, etc. Give the children a range of characters: some healthy, some unfit, some with poor diets. Ask how each one should adapt their lifestyle.

● History: as part of work on the unit 'Children in the Second World War', the class works in role as evacuees and as the families who took in evacuees. They write diaries and letters in role to explore their experiences and feelings. They devise menus for meals that might have been cooked during the war.

● RE: while working on the unit 'Celebrations: Christmas journeys', the children take on the role of Mary and Joseph travelling to Bethlehem. They plan the journey on a map and decide what resources they need to take with them. After this, they take on the characters of the shepherds and the wise men, looking at the journeys these people made and talking about the gifts that they might bring to the Baby Jesus.

You Can... Use the senses to enhance creativity

The very best creative pieces will often appeal to a number of senses simultaneously. A writer might add details of smells and textures, while a composer creates a visual impression through sound.

Thinking points

● Often, lessons appeal to only a limited number of our children's senses – typically their hearing and their sight. The more multi-sensory we can make our approaches to teaching and learning, the more we will encourage our pupils' creative responses.

● Our sense of smell is very strongly associated with lasting memories – you can probably recall the smell of your school canteen from when you were a child! Ironically, this is generally the sense that is least used in educational settings.

● Encourage your pupils to express one sensory experience through the backdrop of another. This will help them learn how to use and develop symbolic and metaphorical representations.

Tips, ideas and activities

● Use different places to encourage your pupils to use their senses. Give a variety of settings, asking the children to brainstorm what they would see, hear, smell, taste and touch in each one. For instance:
  ● the supermarket;
  ● the park;
  ● the beach;
  ● the railway station;
  ● the airport.

● Now use the children's ideas to develop some creative pieces. They might:
  ● use sound effects in drama to create a picture of a place;
  ● create a collage showing the textures of a location;
  ● devise a 'smell experience' where participants sniff a range of items related to a setting.

● Get your pupils to keep a sensory diary, in which they collect sensory experiences that have captured their imaginations. Encourage them to include examples where possible; for instance, a photograph of flowers, a swatch of rough material and so on.

● Take your class on a sensory walk around the school. Heighten the experience by removing some of their senses. For instance, you could blindfold some members of the group, or ask that some children wear earplugs.

● Ask your pupils to describe an impression given by one sense using another. This will help them understand how artists use symbolism to give greater depth to their work. Encourage them to move beyond literal interpretations. They might:
  ● draw the scent of a garden after a rain shower;
  ● use percussion to create a musical picture of a storm;
  ● use language to evoke the textures and smells of a banquet.

● Incorporate the sense of smell into lessons. Ask some children to wear blindfolds and try to identify materials by smell alone. In science, can they locate metal objects? In history, can they say which item is old and which is new?

You Can... Encourage your children to take creative risks

For original, imaginative work to happen, there needs to be an element of risk – of chance, and, the subsequent possibility of failure. In today's society, and particularly in schools, the idea that we must minimise risk has taken hold. It can be hard for us to take risks, but they are essential if we really want to encourage creativity.

Thinking points

● While risk assessments can be valuable, they do discourage us from using our common sense. Even in the most controlled situation, the unexpected can always happen. Thinking creatively helps us respond to unforeseen events.

● Worrying about what others will think can hamper genuine creativity. We need to encourage our children to put aside fears about external judgements of their work, and to have faith and courage in their own ideas.

● The most original creative ideas are often far ahead of what is currently viewed as 'acceptable'. Think, for instance, of the initial reactions to Damien Hirst's shark suspended in a tank of formaldehyde (*The Physical Impossibility of Death in the Mind of Someone Living*, 1991). It can take time for us to see the value of the new and strikingly original, beyond its initial shock factor.

Tips, ideas and activities

● Approach a traditional creative activity from a new direction. Ask your pupils to complete it 'without' the normal resources they would expect to use. This will force them into taking risks and thinking of creative approaches. For instance, you might ask them to:
  ● create a painting without using a paintbrush (they might drip the paint, step in it or find alternative 'brushes' such as leaves or sponges);
  ● make music without using any instruments;
  ● write a story without using the letter 'e';
  ● create a sculpture without using their hands.

● It sounds counter-intuitive, but putting constraints on our creativity can often help free us up to take risks. You could get your pupils to:
  ● write a story using exactly 30 words;
  ● draw a picture made up only of straight lines;
  ● devise a piece of drama in which the characters can only say one word at a time;
  ● create a poem using only 20 given words.

● Mix up the different arts subjects, so that the children are forced to express their ideas in a new way. For example, you might ask the class to:
  ● draw a piece of music as they listen to it;
  ● create a sculpture using their bodies as the material;
  ● tell a story with musical instruments, percussion and sound effects;
  ● make a picture using letters and words rather than images.

● Often, the less time we have to think (and consequently to worry about how others might react), the more creative risks we are willing to take. Show the children an object (for instance, a toy dinosaur) and ask them to:
  ● go straight into an improvisation incorporating it;
  ● take 30 seconds to draw it;
  ● write a poem about it in two minutes.

You Can... **Help your children to make artistic judgements**

Looking at how and why a piece of art 'works' (or does not) is an important factor in understanding how to be creative. Any judgement on creativity is inevitably subjective to a degree. However, there are certain aspects that your pupils will probably agree are important.

Thinking points

● The way our education system is organised can lead children to believe that what is really important is to achieve a finished piece of work. It is vital to challenge this idea if your aim is to look for examples of genuine creativity.

● Looking at a range of pieces created by others can help your pupils develop their own creative work. However, it is also necessary to encourage them to find their personal artistic style or 'voice'.

● Talking about creativity with other children, in a group setting, will help your pupils see that opinions can vary a great deal. This in turn should hopefully give them more confidence about their own creative achievements.

Tips, ideas and activities

● Encourage the children to make judgements about what is 'good' creatively, and why. To do this:

  ○ Collect lots of pupil drawings, paintings, collages and so on – both drafts and finished pieces. These might come from your current class, from previous classes you have taught or from other classes in the school.

  ○ If you are happy to plan ahead, you could gather all the artwork that the children produce over the year, and do this as an end of year activity.

  ○ Create five 'packs' in plastic folders, with about five to ten artworks in each. Aim for a mixture of different styles, materials, finished and unfinished work and so on.

  ○ Give each pack a number from one to five. Give each artwork inside the pack a number or letter for easy reference.

  ○ You might like to include one pack with famous pieces of art; for instance, *Sunflowers* by Van Gogh and *Water Lilies* by Monet.

  ○ Work together to establish a set of criteria for judging whether a piece of art is 'good'. Highlight the importance of imagination and originality, as well as the finished look of a piece.

  ○ Divide the class into groups, circulating the packs around each group in turn.

  ○ For each pack, ask the children to discuss which of the artworks they feel are best. They should award first, second and third position to these.

  ○ You might like to use the photocopiable sheet on page 56 ('What makes a 'good' piece of art?') for the children to record the chosen artwork and their scores.

  ○ When all the groups have looked at each pack, you could get the children to collate the data to discover which picture the class placed first overall.

You Can... Plan lessons that encourage creativity

Planning lessons can sometimes feel like a rather mundane part of the job (until you get the lesson in front of the class, it is hard to bring it to life in your mind). It is the skill of the teacher to plan lessons that encourage and develop creativity, while at the same time covering the relevant curriculum areas.

Thinking points

- The more varied the tasks you use, the more creative your children's responses will tend to be. You will also appeal to children's different learning styles, particularly those who like to take 'hands-on' approaches to their work.

- Even the 'driest' topic can be spiced up by using different approaches; for instance, something as simple as using the children themselves for counting and sorting tasks in maths.

- Another great approach is to incorporate tasks from one area of the curriculum into lessons in another. For instance, you might create a piece of music out of materials that you are studying in science. This kind of cross-disciplinary approach is great for inspiring creative ideas.

Tips, ideas and activities

- When planning a lesson or a scheme of work, keep to hand a copy of the photocopiable sheet on page 57 ('Different kinds of tasks'). You might:
  - use the photocopiable sheet to help you incorporate a good variety of approaches; for instance, setting yourself a target of five different tasks in each lesson;
  - give a copy to other members of staff at your school, to encourage them to use a range of tasks as well;
  - explore how you can use an approach from one area (for example, sculpture in art) to teach a different subject (such as sculpting onomatopoeic words to demonstrate their qualities in English).

- Find ways of incorporating 'hands-on' activities – these offer a great way of reinforcing learning and ensuring that it is memorable. They appeal especially to children who like to learn in a kinaesthetic way. You might:
  - bring in objects for the children to handle, perhaps as part of a scenario set up in class;
  - add textures and lift-up flaps to displays and encourage the children to interact with them;
  - incorporate food into those lessons which are not traditionally associated with cooking (for instance, in a geography lesson, spread butter onto bread to demonstrate population expansion).

- Sometimes, the most creative lessons are those where you have done little formal planning. You might enter the room with an interesting resource, or a challenging question, and allow the children to direct the course of the learning.

- Children respond well to formats that they have seen on television. Consider how you can adapt popular programmes to make a basis for teaching and learning. Quiz shows work particularly well.

You Can... Take your class on an imaginative journey

Any act of creativity is essentially a journey. We begin with some kind of destination in mind (a painting, a story, a subject, an image) and as we travel towards this destination we might take a variety of interesting and imaginative routes or diversions.

Thinking points

● The idea of travelling somewhere new or interesting offers a useful symbolic basis for discussing the imaginative process. It can also be used as a great approach for looking at new places in geography lessons.

● There is something very exciting about going on a journey – for some of your pupils, the imaginative plane trip described here might be their first experience of travelling 'overseas'.

● As well as recreating the flight with your class, you can also take the children on a journey of the imagination that takes place in their minds. Ask the children to close their eyes and talk them into a different place (a forest, a beach). Many children find these imaginative journeys relaxing and also inspirational.

Tips, ideas and activities

● Use the idea of an imaginative trip as an inspiration for some geography or history work. In history, the children might travel back in time. In geography, try this 'flights of fancy' activity for studying an overseas location.

● Use the photocopiable sheet on page 58 ('Passport to the world') as a starting point.

● Get each child to create his or her own passport. Show the class your own passport, talking through the various things that are in it and how it acts as a legal document.

● The children also need to create their aeroplane tickets. Give out a series of letter/number combinations for seat numbers, as on a real flight (A1, A2, A3 and so on).

● Talk about where you are going (for instance, India) – brainstorm with the class to see what they already know, and ask them to do some additional research.

● For added realism, get the children to pack appropriate clothing for their journey and bring it in a small bag to the next lesson.

● Set up an open space as an aeroplane, organising the seats into rows. Label each seat with a corresponding letter/ number.

● Invite the children into the space, 'checking' their passports as they enter (you might get a couple of volunteers to act as 'passport controllers').

● As they enter, the children sit in the seat indicated on their tickets.

● If you are brave enough, do a 'safety demonstration'.

● Simulate a 'take off' – the children slide down in their chairs as the plane takes off. You might also experience some 'turbulence' during the flight!

● On arrival, show a variety of interesting resources – foods, spices, materials, music – to create a multi-sensory experience of reaching a new country.

You Can... Use the media to inspire creativity

Modern children, particularly those living in the western world, are surrounded by the media pretty much from the day that they are born. There are very few children who have not been influenced in some way by the media sources they have seen and heard.

Thinking points

● Because the media is so ubiquitous these days, it is ever more vital for our children to be media savvy. We can help them understand how the media works, and how it can manipulate the way that they think and feel.

● Perhaps one of the most topical media-related issues is that of body image, especially for young girls. Contrast images from celebrity magazines with Dove's Campaign for Real Beauty (see www campaignforrealbeauty.com).

● The almost instant accessibility of global news has created a sense that we live in a 'global society'. But not all news has equal media value – think about the amount of coverage that stories from different parts of the world get.

Tips, ideas and activities

● Do not rule out the radio for media-inspired creativity in the belief that young people prefer visual formats. There has been a big resurgence of interest in the radio, particularly with the advent of digital broadcasting. It is particularly useful for allowing your pupils who have limited literacy to express themselves. You might get the children to:
  ● create a 'jingle' for a radio show;
  ● record a news bulletin or a traffic report;
  ● host an interview with a celebrity guest;
  ● record a sports report, perhaps live from your school sports day.

● Host a 'press conference' in your classroom, with the children playing the parts of journalists, publicists, people involved in the story, etc.

● Get your pupils to create a collage showing how the media can manipulate our thoughts and feelings in a negative and a positive way. For instance, the media can shape how we see:
  ● a celebrity figure, such as David Beckham;
  ● body image, particularly for girls;
  ● brand names;
  ● toys and games, especially around Christmas time.

● Explore the ways in which newspapers use language to hook in and influence their readers. Here are some activities around the idea of influential language:
  ● Get copies of various tabloid and broadsheet newspapers. Cut out various versions of the same story. Ask your pupils to highlight emotive language that is not simply there to tell the story. Talk about the intended impact on the reader.
  ● Show your class a series of different headlines. Working in groups, ask the children to choose one headline and present it in different formats; for instance, as a tabloid newspaper story, as a live news report, as a radio newsflash, and so on.

You Can... **Use constraints to enhance creativity**

It is tempting to believe that being creative is about 'going with the flow' or having no barriers or limits on what you do. Although a sense of freedom is important, it can also lead to a situation where nothing gets done, because 'anything is possible'.

Thinking points

● Giving your pupils constraints or deadlines for a piece of creative work will help get them motivated and on task. It may be particularly useful for those children who are high achievers and perfectionists.

● With fixed limits on what we are allowed to do, or with little time to complete something, concerns about what others will think tend to get put to one side. The urge to get something done can often free up the imagination and silence the critical voice that nags in our minds.

● Children often feel that they should be able to go straight into doing a final piece, without seeing the need for planning and drafting. Gathering lots of rough ideas, sketches and so on will show them how useful these are in making a finished work of art.

Tips, ideas and activities

● There are a multitude of different limits or constraints you might set for your pupils. You can find some ideas below to get you started.

● Setting a time limit is an obvious way of establishing constraints on a piece of work. This might be a limited time, within a lesson (five minutes to do a specific task) or a time limit for when something must be completed (by the end of the lesson).

● In English, word limits can be a very effective way of encouraging creative thinking, and also teaching editing skills. Playing around with words is also very useful for extending vocabulary and learning about how language works. Be very specific about the limits you set, as this teaches the children self-discipline and also forces them to be creative. Refuse to deviate from your constraint, no matter how much the children beg! Here are some possible constraints:

  ● Start with a large number of words (for instance, in a free writing piece) and then ask that the children cut this down to a specified limit.
  ● Give the children a set amount of words (such as 20) with which to tell a story.
  ● Put a limit on the kind of words that are used; for instance, no words that contain the letter 'e', or no words of more than two syllables.
  ● Devise a constraint relating to how sentences are constructed, for example, ask the children to write a piece with no more than five words in each sentence. Examine the effect that this has on how a piece of writing reads.

● In art, you might place limits on the types and quantities of materials that the children use. For instance, ask them to make a drawing using only two colours, or in a single medium.

You Can... Use group work in a creative way

Group work plays an important role in teaching and learning. Using it in an imaginative way can certainly contribute to the overall levels of creativity in your classroom. On the face of it group work would seem to be a relatively easy format to use. However, getting it right can be far trickier than it might at first appear.

Thinking points

● We might turn to group work as a way of encouraging creative thinking and ideas. Certainly, done in the appropriate way, it can provide an excellent format for brainstorming activities.

● During group activities, the children will often take on specific roles, not necessarily ones that are beneficial to the work or to increasing their skills. For instance, one child might often dominate or lead any discussion, while another might typically stay quiet.

● Although group work can seem an ideal format for creative tasks, in real life examples of creativity (film making, theatre) there is usually one person in charge of directing the activity.

Tips, ideas and activities

● Set some group tasks in which very clear parameters and constraints are given. This will often make for a much more focused, inclusive and creative approach. For instance, you might ask that:
  ● everyone gives one idea in turn;
  ● the children use an object, such as a 'conch' (as in *Lord of the Flies*), to indicate whose turn it is to speak;
  ● the groups only have three minutes to brainstorm ideas.

● Try using the 'doughnut' approach when doing group work tasks. This is a great method for getting everyone to share their ideas. Here is how it works:
  ● Set up a group task. Ask each group to choose one volunteer to be a spokesperson.
  ● At the end of a specified time, stop the groups and get the spokespeople to move to the next group.
  ● Each spokesperson talks to the new group about the ideas which they have devised.
  ● Afterwards, the spokespeople might go back to their original groups, or stay where they are, perhaps moving on to a further group after the next part of the task.
  ● This approach works really well in an ICT lesson. After the children have been working on a task for a while, each child moves on one seat to comment on someone else's work.

● Get the children to wear different 'hats' to indicate the contribution they will make. You might use the 'thinking hats' approach described on page 23 ('Use colour to inspire creativity'). You could use a selection of different hats that you have available, talking with the children about the relevant approach. For instance:
  ● a baseball cap for someone who bounces ideas around;
  ● a police helmet for someone who 'polices' the discussion;
  ● a builder's hard hat for someone who helps build the ideas;
  ● a magician's hat for someone who gives innovative suggestions.

You Can... Make a creative classroom space

Classroom spaces vary hugely between schools, and even within the same school there can be a range of different settings. The style, layout and atmosphere of your classroom can have a direct influence on the learning that your pupils do within the space, so it pays to think creatively.

Thinking points

● Even if you are stuck with a dismal classroom space, there is still plenty you can do to adapt and change it for the better. In doing so, you will be using your own creative talents, and making daily life better for your pupils.

● Sometimes, classrooms change little from year to year, or from teacher to teacher. Habit, routine and tradition created by a space, can get in the way of innovative thinking.

● Do not be afraid to make changes if you do not like the way that your room feels. If a classroom has looked a particular way for a long time, this is perhaps all the more reason to change it.

Tips, ideas and activities

The following steps will help you develop a teaching space which encourages creative teaching and learning:

● First, stand back and take an overview of your space. Try to look at it as someone who has just stepped into the room. What strikes you first? What is good? What needs changing?

● Make a list of any practical issues. Is it tricky to reach certain parts of the room? Do you bump into desks?

● Identify 'fixed' items which you will have to work around, such as heaters and electronic whiteboards. Consider whether there are any unusual solutions to dealing with these.

● Think outside the box – often the best ideas will seem a bit crazy at first. Do not rule out anything unusual or tricky at this stage.

● Think about different dimensions in your room. Can you do anything with the walls, ceiling or floors (for instance, adding shelves for storage)?

● Explore potential changes of direction. Would it work to turn the entire focus of the space around?

● Consider your use of colour, shape and texture and how this could be developed.

● Sit in each seat to look at the room. This helps you understand the space from the children's perspective.

● Create a sample layout on paper, cutting out shapes for desks, chairs, etc to experiment before moving anything for real.

● Enlist the help of a friendly caretaker or TA to help you make any changes.

You Can... Incorporate creativity into routine activities

Our lives (both in school and at home) are often dictated by routines: what time we get up, what we have for breakfast, the journey into school and so on. Incorporating creativity into our routines can help us add a bit of spice to our daily lives.

Thinking points
● There are plenty of routine tasks that teachers have to do daily or weekly in their classrooms. Often these take up a fair amount of time during the average school day – time that could be spent in a creative manner.

● Although routines are great for getting your pupils to work and behave in a focused way, too much structure can dampen our creative instincts and lead to a sense of boredom. Have a think regularly about how you might adapt your routines, perhaps once every half term, to keep your pupils on their toes.

● By approaching routine activities in an imaginative way, you should boost the role and status of creativity in your classroom. You can also have a lot of fun with your pupils, thinking up new and innovative ways of doing mundane jobs.

Tips, ideas and activities
● Play around with the way that you take the register, to keep your pupils on their toes and to encourage creative thinking and imaginative responses. You might:
  ● take the register backwards (a particularly beneficial approach for the child whose name is last on the list and who probably ends up at the back of the line in many routine activities at school);
  ● ask the children to do something (stand up, make a gesture or a noise) when they hear their names;
  ● get the class to reply in another language;
  ● sing the names as an opera, as a rap or in the style of a heavy metal song.

● When you are going from one part of the school to another (for instance, for assembly), get the children to move in an interesting, imaginative way. For example, they could walk:
  ● in slow motion;
  ● as though they are in zero gravity;
  ● as if they are trudging through mud;
  ● in the manner of a police officer, an elderly person, a monster…

● There are plenty of times when you might need to line up the class; for instance, when going out to and coming in from break. Spice things up by devising a variety of different ways of making a line. You might ask the children to line up:
  ● in height order;
  ● in reverse height order;
  ● in order of their birth dates (give them a bit of time for this, as it is tricky to organise);
  ● facing and walking backwards;
  ● in alphabetical order of their first names (again, give them some time to organise this).

You Can... Use colour to inspire creativity

It only takes a brief walk in a garden full of colourful flowers to demonstrate how many feelings colour can evoke in us. Throughout the ages, artists working in various creative disciplines have been inspired by and have used colour to create powerful responses in those who have seen their work.

Thinking points

● Different colours can evoke a whole range of emotions, sensory responses and associations. The conceptual understanding of these symbolic links is an important step in the development of thinking skills.

● Using colour is a great way to inspire and encourage creativity in your classroom, not only in displays, but also in posters, lessons, reward systems and so on.

● Colours are also useful in helping teachers explain and express different kinds of thinking. Edward de Bono developed the now widely used idea of 'six thinking hats' to show how this can be done.

Tips, ideas and activities

● Use the 'thinking hats' approach for problem-solving activities. Create six coloured hats for your pupils (this could be done using coloured paper, or you might buy some cheap coloured baseball caps). Divide the class into groups to discuss a topic, asking each group to wear and think via one of the hats. For more information about this approach, you might like to look at: www.edwdebono.com

● Colours can offer a great way of creating more interesting reward and sanction systems. For instance, you might have:
  - Robert the red pen – a pen that the children get to use for working well;
  - bronze, silver and gold certificates for good work or behaviour;
  - coloured cards to indicate working well (green), first warning (orange), serious issues (red);
  - a rainbow on the wall, with a Velcro®-backed sun symbol – if the children are working well, the sun moves upwards and vice versa.

● Do not rule out more graphic approaches to colour – often a pure black and white display can be visually more striking than a variety of other colours. A simple two-tone effect is especially useful for highlighting information, for instance, during a topic on newspaper headlines.

● Try to get a range of the colour swatches that are used to show different paint colours in DIY stores. You might use these for:
  - inspiring discussion about how different colours make us feel during some speaking and listening work;
  - in an art lesson, looking at how some colours clash and others work well together, or at different shades and tones;
  - showing the children a variety of colours and asking what they symbolise: red is for 'stop'; green is for 'go' and so on.

You Can... **Use resources to develop creativity**

Children do love to get 'hands-on' with resources and equipment. There is something about being able to handle an object during a lesson that makes the learning far more likely to 'stick'. The more unusual the resources you have available, the more likely you are to encourage creativity in your classroom.

Thinking points

● It is tempting to believe that to appeal to children, your resources need to be the more sophisticated, bought-in materials. In fact, it is often the simplest objects (a cardboard box, a jar full of paperclips) that inspire the greatest creativity.

● Getting creative with resources is more about how you introduce and use an item, than about what the item actually is. See the 'paperclip' idea below for an example of how this can work.

● Imagining that one object is another, or looking for links between two objects, is an important step in developing an understanding of how metaphor works (for example, looking at how a rock might indicate solidity and trust).

Tips, ideas and activities

● The idea that one (often simple) object can symbolise something else was approached in a really creative way by one school in America. While studying the Holocaust, the children saw how paperclips were worn as a symbol of protest against the Nazis. They decided to collect six million paperclips, as a way of understanding the enormity of the loss of life. To learn more about their project, see:
  ● www.marionschools.org/holocaust/beginninghol.htm
  ● www.acfnewsource.org/religion/paper_clip_project.html

● Share the paperclip story with your class. Then gather some simple resources, and challenge the children to think up their own creative ideas about how an object could symbolise something else. For instance, you might show them:
  ● an empty glass or bottle;
  ● a blanket or piece of fabric;
  ● a ring;
  ● some bamboo canes.

● Look at how in recent years, ribbons, bracelets and other charms have been used in a symbolic way, and also in religions throughout the centuries. For instance, the yellow ribbon symbolises hope of a homecoming. For more information, you might like to look at:
  ● http://news.bbc.co.uk/1/hi/special_report/29436.stm
  ● http://en.wikipedia.org/wiki/Yellow_ribbon

● Examine your resources, and consider how you might use them in unusual, creative ways, rather than as was originally intended. For instance, you might use a set of dictionaries for a 'word pick' game. Get the children to open a dictionary at a random page and pick one word, repeat until you have a set of words and then use them to create an unusual sentence or story.

● The internet is a great resource for ideas. The Woodlands School site offers a very useful set of resource links (see www.woodlands-junior.kent.sch.uk/Teacher.html).

You Can... **Design and build creative displays**

If you look in a typical classroom, the display work on the walls is often highly creative and artistic. It is one area of the job where teachers, support staff and children can really let their imaginations run riot. Finding some more unusual ways to create displays, will help you express your artistic talents even further.

Thinking points

● It sounds obvious, but when putting up displays, bear in mind the height of your pupils. If the displays are literally 'above their heads', they are far less likely to look at and interact with them.

● I have found that displays can often be overlooked by children, even when they are eye-catching and beautifully presented. It is worth giving the children a bit of lesson time in which to look at the displays, ask questions, make comments and so on.

● We sometimes view displays as a way of showing the 'end result' of a topic or piece of work. However, using displays in more unusual, creative ways can reinvigorate the way that the children see them.

Tips, ideas and activities

● Create some 'display spaces' loosely based on the idea of Tracey Emin's famous tent. There is something very intimate and interesting about going inside a small space to see what is inside. You might use a real tent, or create a kind of wigwam effect using a piece of material hung from the ceiling.

● Displays can often seem quite flat, and consequently rather uninspiring. Think in three dimensions when planning displays. You could:
  ● put a table in front of a display, with related objects on it for the children to handle;
  ● create pop-out or pop-up images to add to a flat display.

● Get inventive with where you actually put your displays. Look around your room with fresh eyes to see the possibilities, and ask your children for their ideas. Here are some suggestions:
  ● You might use the ceilings for displaying work – hang up a washing line with pegs or pin strings to the ceiling tiles so that they hang down just above your head.
  ● If you have an unusual structural feature in your room, such as a column or a beam, think of ways that you could use this for display work.
  ● Do not forget the floor – you could tape some lines as part of work on measurement or pin down a piece of soft fabric to create a comfy area for reading.

● Rather than always having static displays, use the idea of a 'working wall' – this is a display to which you and the children add as the work progresses. For instance, in science, you might start with a simple outline diagram, then get the children to add colour, then labels and finally examples of research or work.

You Can... Encourage creativity among staff

There's a well-known saying: 'the family that plays together, stays together'. In much the same way, where the staff of an organisation (whether a school or a business) feel relaxed, happy and creative, they are far more likely to remain dedicated to their work.

Thinking points

- Creative thinking and imaginative approaches are especially useful when it comes to problem solving. Where school staff are used to taking innovative ideas on board, this can really help when problems do arise.

- The sense that we personally can be creative and innovative at work plays a key part in helping us feel connected to an organisation. This in turn helps with staff morale, retention and recruitment.

- As part of a more traditional INSET schedule, incorporate some opportunities for the staff to get creative together. This is a great way of rewarding hard work, building a sense of camaraderie and also inspiring imaginative approaches.

Tips, ideas and activities

- Hold some creative competitions among staff. Where appropriate, get the children involved in the judging process. This is a great way of encouraging the staff to get creative, and also of rewarding the work of those who regularly make an effort beyond the call of duty. You could:
  - give regular prizes for 'most creative' or 'best' classroom displays, perhaps once every half term;
  - hold a competition for planting up a container with flowers or vegetables to put in the playground;
  - try a 'grow the tallest sunflower' competition, perhaps allowing children as well as staff to take part;
  - hold a competition to devise a new school slogan, design a new uniform, or landscape part of the school grounds;
  - host an 'after hours' (that is, no pupils allowed) staff competition for singing or dancing.

- There are often plenty of opportunities for the children to perform at school. Why not set up a similar tradition of staff performances for the children? In the past, I have taken part in several staff pantomimes presented to the children at Christmas time. Although this involves a fair bit of work, there are many advantages to be had:
  - The cast and crew have great fun producing, rehearsing and performing the show.
  - The children really appreciate the chance to see teachers and other staff making a bit of a fool of themselves.
  - It is important for promoting creativity for the children to see staff taking part in creative ventures.
  - It is a great way to keep yourself happy and motivated during the dark winter months, and to finish the term on a high note.
  - The 'afterglow' of a good reputation with the children can be hugely beneficial in your classroom after the event.

You Can... Use meeting time in a creative way

Teachers (and other school staff) are busy people. Consequently, it is very frustrating for them if they feel that meeting time is not well spent. While we would never dream of sitting our pupils down and talking at them for an hour, this approach often prevails in staff meetings.

Thinking points

● Taking a creative approach in meetings might mean slightly less time for getting through documents and policies, but it should mean that staff feel more engaged with this aspect of school life.

● Allowing staff to feed back their ideas is important for creating a sense of ownership, particularly when school policies are being changed or developed.

● It can sometimes be tricky to find a balance between allowing questions and feedback, and a meeting simply turning into a moaning session. Be specific about how and when feedback will happen, set a time limit and find ways to ensure that everyone can contribute.

Tips, ideas and activities

● Whenever possible, format and deliver your meetings like a good lesson. The approaches we use with children are just as important for engaging an audience of staff. For instance, you might try to make meetings:
  ● appeal to different learning styles – kinaesthetic as well as visual and auditory;
  ● interactive – inviting feedback, allowing discussion time, asking for opinions and so on;
  ● visually interesting – for example, through the use of diagrams, PowerPoint®, mind maps, and so on.

● It can be hard for staff to give honest opinions if they feel they are going to be put on the spot about their ideas. Use an anonymous feedback system such as a post box, ideas bag or suggestions board to overcome this.

● Consider using some meeting time in an alternative way to the traditional 'sit down and listen' format. For instance, you might use it to help all the staff learn more about how the school works, or to share examples of good practice. You could:
  ● ask the staff to go on a tour of the school to see what happens in the different classrooms and other spaces, such as the office;
  ● set a challenge, such as asking staff to go around the school to find an example of a really good display, and then feed back on this at the end of the meeting;
  ● invite teachers to give a short demonstration lesson to the rest of the staff, perhaps on a topic or activity that has worked particularly well;
  ● get some visitors into the school to give a short talk or demonstration during a staff meeting;
  ● do something aimed at improving staff morale and a sense of well-being – a circus skills workshop, a yoga class or an Indian head massage session.

You Can... Devise creative assemblies

Assemblies play a vital role in creating a sense of community within a school and, done properly, they can be exciting learning experiences. Look around the hall at your children's faces and ask yourself whether they are really engaged with what is going on. If not, consider taking more creative approaches to assembly time.

Thinking points

● There can be a tendency in some schools for assemblies to be run in a rather traditional way, with a specific format that varies little from year to year. This is a shame – taking a more creative approach towards assembly time can mean it becomes a far more engaging and exciting part of school life.

● As a rare time when the whole school comes together, assemblies offer a great opportunity for the children to participate in creative activities as a group. This allows the younger children to learn from and be inspired by the efforts of the older ones, and vice versa.

Tips, ideas and activities

● Consider how you might create a more interesting, imaginative entrance to and exit from your assembly. Here are some ideas:

  ● Choose a piece of music with a specific word in mind (an emotion, image, theme or topic). Write the word on a slip of paper and seal it in an envelope. During the assembly, invite the children to guess what the word might be and give a prize for the correct answer.

  ● Ask the children to enter the hall or assembly space in a particular way; for instance, 'in the style of' a verb such as 'trudge', or an adverb such as 'fearfully'.

  ● If you are presenting an assembly, find ways to make a 'splash' when you come in. For example, you could enter on a skateboard or a bike for a talk on road safety.

  ● Use costumes, accessories or props for added visual interest.

● Consider whether your assembly space could be used in a more creative way. This will help work against the sense of routine which can accompany assemblies. For instance, you could:

  ● turn the focus around, so that the children face in the opposite direction;

  ● if your children sit on the floor for assembly, let them sit on chairs occasionally, and vice versa;

  ● change the adults' position in the room – for instance, getting teachers to sit with someone else's class;

  ● when presenting an assembly, play around with your position (for instance, sitting on a desk or standing on a podium).

● Get the children to take part in a creative activity together during the assembly. For instance, they could make a huge collage or mural related to the assembly topic.

● For more ideas and activities, the website www.assemblies.org.uk is a great resource.

You Can... **Enhance the creativity of your outdoor spaces**

Getting out in the fresh air can be a great way to get the creative juices flowing. Whether it is a quick walk around the playground, or a longer topic based on the natural world, there is a whole range of sensory and learning experiences that can take place in the great outdoors.

Thinking points

● Those lessons that take place outdoors are often the ones that the children remember best. There seems to be something about the multi-sensory nature of the outside world that helps their brains retain the information.

● There are many obvious ways in which you can use the outdoors for science-related work. But taking your class outside can also provide a way to inspire learning in poetry, dance, drama, art, history and so on.

● Where there are opportunities for creativity in the playground and outdoor spaces, this can often help minimise any behaviour issues during break times. The more chance the children have to express themselves, the less likely they are to think about messing around.

Tips, ideas and activities

● Find ways to get your children exploring and interacting with the outdoor spaces at your school. You might:
  ● set up a treasure hunt in the school grounds – you can vary this according to the season, for instance, an Easter egg hunt or a spooky Halloween hunt;
  ● create a nature trail, asking the children to find and perhaps photograph different creatures and plants, answer questions and so on;
  ● place a series of clues around the grounds, perhaps linked to a science topic you are studying in class, and then ask your children to act as detectives to find them;
  ● bury some objects in the ground or in a sandpit and get your class to work as archaeologists to dig them up.

● Get your class working outside as often as you can – getting 'hands-on' with the natural world can lead to some great creativity – not just in science-related topics, but also for imaginative writing and so on.

● If your school does not already have a garden area, why not put a team together and plant some flowers or vegetables? Learning how to sow seeds, grow plants and make compost can lead to some fantastic learning experiences. Some schools even keep farm animals in their outdoor spaces.

● Consider adding some designs to the playground surfaces – as well as the traditional hopscotch pattern, you might also incorporate some shapes, puzzle grids, wavy lines, and so on. The more generic these are, the more creative the children will be in the way that they use them.

● For some stunning wooden furniture, sculptures and play equipment, have a look at www.handmadeplaces.co.uk. Even if your school budget does not run to this kind of equipment, it might give you some ideas.

You Can... Offer your children a range of creative experiences

With the advent of the literacy and numeracy strands in recent years, there has been less and less time available in the school day to devote to creative projects. In many schools, the entire morning has been given over to 'the basics', with an inevitable impact on the time available for other subject areas.

Thinking points

- Creative experiences can encompass a whole range of things. As well as the traditional arts subjects (dance, drama, music, art), other areas such as gardening and design technology can offer many creative opportunities.

- For students who struggle with the basics, school must sometimes seem like a very difficult place to be. By allowing children to express themselves, and to let off a bit of creative steam, we can hopefully re-engage them with the idea that learning is fun and exciting.

- Although the basics are clearly important, it is a worry that we are creating a generation of children who get very little time for creative activity during the normal school day.

Tips, ideas and activities

- Bring plenty of visitors into the school to get involved in creative activities with the children. This is perhaps especially important if yours is a small school with only a few teachers. You could invite:
  - arts students from a nearby secondary school, sixth form or FE college;
  - local writers or poets;
  - parents who are experts on various creative subjects.

- A vibrant extra-curricular 'scene' in a school is a good indicator of staff morale. A lunchtime or after-school club can offer opportunities to extend the curriculum beyond what is possible in lessons. To ease the load on staff in smaller schools, ask whether volunteers (parents, local people) might be able to run an activity.

- If you currently only put on one school show per year (probably a nativity play), consider whether you might add an additional date or two. Put the main onus on the children for devising the performance. You might set up a dance competition, a music evening and so on.

- The more you can get your children involved in adding their creative touches to the school, the more likely they are to respect and enjoy their environment. They might:
  - create a mosaic version of the school badge or crest;
  - be given an 'art wall' in the playground on which to paint designs;
  - design a reward postcard for teachers to use as part of the behaviour system;
  - plant and care for a small garden area in the school grounds.

- Consider holding a 'collapse' or 'break-out' day at your school. This is a day on which the normal timetable is suspended. During the day, children of all ages work together on cross-curricular projects around a central theme.

You Can... **Use the weather to inspire creativity**

In the UK, the weather is a source of pretty much constant inspiration. For a start, it changes so quickly, sometimes even during a single day. You need only look up into the sky to be inspired by cloud formations, different kinds of light and so on.

Thinking points

● The weather and the seasons provide a great basis for experimenting with imagery. You can use them to introduce and reinforce terms such as personification, simile and even pathetic fallacy.

● Many of the great creative geniuses have been inspired by the weather: Van Gogh's tormented skies, Monet's sunlit pools, Wordsworth's beautiful images of the Lake District.

● There is of course a clear link between the weather and our emotions – every teacher knows just how awkward a class can be on a wild, wet and windy day. Use these emotional responses to help inspire creative activities in your classroom.

Tips, ideas and activities

● Use the weather and the seasons to play around with imagery, getting the children to focus on their sensory responses. For example:

   ● simile: 'That summer was as hot and steamy as a sauna.'
   ● simile: 'The thunder crashed like cymbals in the sky.'
   ● metaphor: 'Winter laid a blanket of white over the land.'
   ● personification: 'The clouds threw icy fingers of hail to the ground.'

● You might ask the children to:
   ● draw a picture to describe the image;
   ● devise some of their own weather-related images;
   ● write a story or devise a drama in which the characters are various kinds of weather.

● Get your class to make weather sounds using percussion instruments, their bodies, and any other resources they can get their hands on. Ask the children to devise a storm soundtrack, then record, listen to and evaluate it.

● Introduce the term 'pathetic fallacy' to your class. Although this is a fairly advanced literary concept, children in Key Stage 2 can understand how it works. Pathetic fallacy describes the technique of using the weather to mirror the action in a story. For instance, in Jane Eyre, at a climactic moment in the story there is a violent storm and a tree is split in half by lightning. This mirrors the violent emotions of the characters and the breakdown of the relationship between Jane and Rochester.

You Can... Get creative with the seasons

Throughout the centuries, artists working in many different art forms have taken inspiration from the landscape, and from the way that it changes over the course of the year. Making connections with the natural world and its wonders, whatever the season, is a great way to inspire creativity.

Thinking points

● The different seasons inspire a very different kind of 'feeling' and creative response. Spring has the sense of new life, and things about to happen, whereas autumn is a time when things start to ripen and decay, and the year begins to draw to a close.

● Watching how the seasons change the view from the classroom window is a good way to help your pupils understand the passing of time. This concept can be very tricky for younger children to grasp – for them, time seems to have a peculiarly elastic quality.

● The celebrations that mark the course of the year are closely linked to the season within which they happen. Thus we have the springtime eggs at Easter, or the autumn fruiting pumpkins at Halloween.

Tips, ideas and activities

● Use the photocopiable sheet on page 59 ('Changing seasons') to make a flick book showing how the landscape changes through the seasons. Here is what your pupils should do:
  ● Colour in each of the pictures, perhaps using a slightly different shade in each one, to show the gradual changes over the course of the year.
  ● Cut out each of the pictures and join them together in the correct order. This can be done using staples or sticky tape.
  ● Some children could use this activity as the inspiration for creating a longer flick book of their own.

● Use other creative approaches to show how the landscape changes from one season to the next. Your pupils could:
  ● take a series of digital photographs across the course of the school year;
  ● use the 'slideshow' format on a website such as http://photobucket.com to animate these;
  ● create a series of collages of the same scene, showing how it looks in each season;
  ● devise a piece of music to echo the changes in the 'feel' of each season;
  ● create a dance based around the idea of the changing seasons.

● Explore the ways in which poets and writers have made symbolic links between the passing of the seasons and the course of human life. Talk together about why these connections might have been made.

● Read 'Ode to Autumn', by John Keats, with your class. Although your children might find some of the language difficult, they should be able to pick out certain striking images from the poem, perhaps using these to inspire seasonal poetry of their own.

You Can... Get experimental at Christmas time

Christmas is traditionally a time when a great deal of creativity is going on in classrooms up and down the country. Although traditional creative activities are great fun, you could also see Christmas as a time when you can go a bit crazy and do some interesting experiments with your class.

Thinking points

● For many children, the main focus at Christmas has become the giving and especially receiving of presents. Exploring creative ways to celebrate the traditions of Christmas should hopefully inspire them to remember that it is about more than just commerce.

● There are many symbols which play a key role in the Christmas celebrations. Exploring what these symbols are, and the various meanings that they can have, will help your pupils understand the creative use of imagery.

● The dark nights and coloured lights of Christmas mean that it can feel like a really magical time. Add to this the beautiful sound of Christmas carols, and you have a recipe for the term to end with a feeling of wonder and imagination.

Tips, ideas and activities

● Get your pupils to try out some creative ideas for retelling the nativity story, perhaps incorporating the best ideas into your Christmas school play. They could tell it:
  ● from a different point of view, for instance, with one of the sheep telling its version;
  ● in an unusual medium; for example, using *Wallace and Gromit*-style animation, or as a cartoon;
  ● in a different form; for instance, as an opera or a rap.

● Experiment with more unusual ways of decorating your Christmas tree. You might try:
  ● coloured feathers, ribbons and sequins;
  ● a single colour theme, such as white or black;
  ● biscuits cut into various shapes and decorated; for instance, iced holly shapes;
  ● a 'Christmas Overseas' theme, perhaps set in Australia, with spiders, snakes, koalas and corks;
  ● a natural approach, using only materials found outdoors, such as pine cones, dried leaves and flowers.

● Spend a lesson experimenting with different stylish and imaginative ways of wrapping up presents:
  ● Get some boxes and containers in various different shapes.
  ● Provide a range of different materials for wrapping, including paper, fabric, ribbons, glitter, etc.
  ● Encourage your children to make some wrapping paper of their own, by using printing techniques.
  ● Explore creative ideas for shapes; for instance, making a cracker out of a bottle-shaped container.

● Make use of the dark afternoons by getting your pupils to experiment with some lighting effects. They might string fairy lights in the bare branches of a tree, or design, create and devise uses for a star curtain. (A star curtain could be made by making small holes in a piece of black cloth and shining lights from behind.)

You Can... Use the months of the year for creativity

Many poets, lyricists and writers have used the months of the year to inspire their work. There is the sense that each month has a different tone or feel to it, whether it is the fresh start promised by January, or the cold, dark days of November.

Thinking points

● The way that the school year runs is still based on a fairly ancient pattern in which children would have helped with the harvest during the long, hot summer.

● The recent introductions of five or six terms in some areas of the country have been aimed at balancing out the spread of holidays across the year.

● Although we traditionally associate certain months of the year with particular celebrations, such as, Halloween and Christmas, other months tend to get overlooked.

● Using the months as a framework for creative activities can be a good way to mark the passage of time and to inspire your pupils.

Tips, ideas and activities

● Explore and analyse some of the songs and poems that have been written featuring various months of the year; discuss the links that artists make to the time of the year. For instance:
  ● 'January' (Pilot);
  ● 'November' (Guns 'N' Roses);
  ● 'October' (Dylan Thomas).

● The poem 'The Months', by Sara Coleridge, provides a useful starting point for creative activities.

● Try this fun idea for renaming the months of the year, getting your pupils to come up with their own ideas for what each month should be called (see www.halfbakery.com/idea/Virtuous_20Months).

● There is an old Wall Street stock market saying, 'Sell in May and go away' (as the stock market is stronger between November and April). Use this as the inspiration for a series of sayings based around the months of the year. These might not necessarily rhyme (January could be tricky!) but they should be related to what might happen in each month.

● Use the tradition of naming the full moons in each month as a basis for some creative activities. (The full moon in January is known as 'Old Moon' in English, 'Wolf Moon' in Native American and 'Paush Purnima' in Hindi, while April's moon is known as 'Egg Moon', 'Pink Moon' and 'Hanuman Jayanti' respectively. You might:
  ● Discuss as a class some of the associations we make with a full moon, for instance, the folklore about werewolves and the association with madness (hence 'lunacy' from 'lunar').
  ● Talk in groups about why they think these names were chosen in the past for full moons.
  ● Devise some modern full moon names.
  ● Create a story in which the full moon plays a key part.
  ● Explore creative ways of drawing the word 'moon' and related images.
  ● Write a full moon poem.

You Can... **Encourage creativity during the holidays**

With an ever more crowded school day, we need to encourage our children to take every possible opportunity to be creative. The school holidays are one obvious time when there is more space and chance for imaginative activities.

Thinking points

● For adults, free time is a very precious resource; for children, it can be hard to think how to fill up holiday time with anything of value. 'I'm bored!' is the classic cry that every parent dreads.

● Sometimes, doing nothing is very valuable, as it gives us a chance to recharge our batteries. Down time can also be great for creativity, because it gives the mind time to wander and can often be a time when inspiration strikes.

● For some of your pupils, every holiday will offer an opportunity to visit new places, experience other cultures and see wonderful sights. For those not lucky enough to be taken away during holiday time, your guidance as to potential creative activities could prove invaluable.

Tips, ideas and activities

● As a class, research the various opportunities that there are in your local area for cultural or creative activities. If you teach in an inner city environment, there are probably plenty of options available. But even in a rural location, there might be gardens that the children could visit, or arts events and workshops run by local organisations. Encourage the children to feed back on at least one creative experience when they return from holiday.

● Use the idea of packing to go on holiday to encourage creative thinking in your pupils. You might ask your pupils to consider:
  ● what various story characters would pack for a holiday; for instance, Tracy Beaker or Alex Rider;
  ● the top five most important items they would want if stranded on a desert island, lost on the top of a mountain, or stuck in an icy wilderness.

● When the sun is shining, most children love to play outside. But keeping yourself entertained on a rainy day is much harder. Get your pupils to brainstorm ten ideas for a wet day at home, the more unusual or imaginative the better.

● Put a world map on the wall. Blindfold a volunteer and ask him/her to put a pin in the map. Now get the whole class to research this location as a holiday destination, perhaps producing a tourist leaflet. Of course, some creative thinking may be required, especially if the pin is stuck in an unusual location (the middle of the ocean, for instance).

You Can... Play around with sound

Sound plays a key part in various artistic disciplines, whether it is percussive and melodic sounds in music, sound effects in a drama or film, or sounds made by language in a piece of writing. Encouraging your pupils to experiment in using sounds will help them give depth and interest to their creative work.

Thinking points

- Children do love to make noise! It is a great way for them to let off steam, and it can also lead to some very creative ventures.

- As a teacher, it can feel both exciting and nerve-racking to allow your class to experiment with sound. There can be a perception that a lot of noise means a lack of work. As long as the noise is focused, and it does not become excessive, this perception is generally a mistaken one.

- Encourage your pupils to explore the counterbalance between sound and silence, and the way that one offsets the other. You might ask for a period of still and silent contemplation at the start or end of a particularly noisy lesson.

Tips, ideas and activities

- Investigate the way that sounds occur in nature, and the feelings that various sounds inspire in us. For instance:
  - plant sounds – shaking seed heads, rustling grasses;
  - sounds made by water – the babbling of a brook, the rushing of a waterfall, the gentle dripping of rain;
  - interacting with natural materials – crunching across gravel, crushing dry leaves, squelching through mud.

- Get your children to experiment with the sounds that they can make with their bodies without, for instance:
  - clicking fingers;
  - clapping hands;
  - humming;
  - whistling;
  - tapping.

- Play a short piece of film with the sound down, and challenge your children to add noises and sound effects. This works particularly well with cartoons and animations.

- Try this drama activity, in which the whole class works together to create a machine with sound effects:
  - Divide the class into groups – each group will be one part of a large machine.
  - Get each group to create a series of mechanised movements with their bodies which link together; for instance, cogs turning, pistons sliding and so on.
  - Now ask them to add some appropriate sound effects.
  - Join the groups together to create a huge machine.

- Play around with words to see the various effects that can be created. Your pupils might:
  - experiment with different animal sounds;
  - repeat a single syllable over and over again;
  - try various 'rounds' (such as 'Row your boat');
  - dramatise a poem which features alliteration.

You Can... Use props to inspire your children

There is something wonderfully inspirational for children (and indeed adults) about having an item or object to work with, particularly one that is not normally seen in the classroom. Often, it is the simplest objects (a cardboard box, a bunch of twigs) which encourage the most creative responses.

Thinking points

● You can incorporate props into many areas of teaching and learning. Whenever you think up an activity for the classroom, consider whether there is some kind of object which would bring it to life.

● Props appeal particularly to those children who like to learn in a 'hands-on' and kinaesthetic way. The simple act of handling and working with an object can focus their attention, encourage them to concentrate and keep them on task.

● It does not have to be complicated or costly to incorporate props into your teaching. A quick look around your home will probably elicit an array of weird and wonderful objects that could be incorporated into your lesson.

Tips, ideas and activities

● Try some circle activities to get your children using props in an interesting way. For instance, you could:
  ● pass an empty cardboard box around, as though there was something in it, such as a heavy weight, a wild animal or a fragile vase;
  ● repeat the activity, but this time with an invisible box;
  ● put a stick in the centre of the circle. Challenge the children to come into the middle and use the stick in an interesting way.

● Use this drama activity to encourage your children to think creatively and to be imaginative about the way that they use props:
  ● Divide the class into small groups.
  ● Give each group a series of simple items – for instance, a sheet of plain A3 paper, an empty cardboard box, a bundle of twigs, an empty plastic bottle.
  ● Ask the children to devise a short scene incorporating all of the props.
  ● Now get them to devise another scene; this time they should use all the props but *not* as they were intended. For example, the A3 paper could be used as a raft or a hat, but it cannot be used as a piece of paper.
  ● Ask each group to decide which scenario was more interesting.
  ● Watch the groups perform their scenes, and talk about why it might be more creative to use a prop in a different way than was intended.

● Use a prop to inspire a story, by putting something in your classroom while the children are at break. Ask the children to devise a character using the prop as a starting point. For instance, someone might have left behind:
  ● an ancient-looking key;
  ● a suitcase filled with interesting items;
  ● a packet of photos.

You Can... Get creative with shapes

Shapes appear everywhere in the artistic disciplines, and indeed in all the curriculum subjects. In art, the relationship between different shapes will create an effective composition. In dance, the shapes made by the dancers' bodies become a key part of the performance.

Thinking points

● There are many possible links between the use of shapes in the arts, and learning about shapes in subjects such as maths and science.

● Adding a three-dimensional aspect to a piece (for instance, by the use of pop-ups) can create a very powerful effect. This is a very useful technique for making displays more engaging and interactive.

● Teachers use shape a great deal in classroom management, as well as in lesson delivery. This is often done in a subconscious way – for instance, rearranging the shape that the furniture makes in the room, or moving around the space in a circle.

Tips, ideas and activities

● As a warm-up for PE (dance) or a drama session, challenge your pupils to make a variety of shapes with their bodies. They could work:
  ● in pairs to create letters or numbers;
  ● in small groups to make a word;
  ● as a class to create a sentence.

● Use this whole-class activity to encourage cooperation and quick thinking:
  ● Ask the children to stand in a space on their own.
  ● Call out a shape (circle, triangle, square, hexagon and so on).
  ● When you say 'go', the children must get into pairs or groups to create the shape you have called.
  ● To 'win', all members of the class must participate – no one should be left out.
  ● Once the children get the hang of it, challenge them to make one shape as a whole class.

● Take your class outside to experiment with creating shapes in the natural world. The children could:
  ● scrape shapes in the ground or in a patch of sand;
  ● look at the shapes within various natural objects, such as leaves, flowers and insects;
  ● design shapes using natural materials (for instance, patterns made with stones);
  ● collect materials with interesting shapes to create a natural mosaic.

● Get your pupils to look at how the shapes in the world around us can be represented in an abstract way. Here are some ideas:
  ● Set up a still life and ask the children to create a collage of it, using simple shapes cut out from coloured paper.
  ● Ask the children to devise a dance piece based around shapes and patterns made on the floor. You might dictate the shapes that you would like used (for example, one circle, two squares, three triangles).
  ● Get them to write a series of shape poems.

You Can... **Use textures in a creative way**

'Texture' can mean various things in the different artistic fields. In art, it might refer to the feel of a material that is being used; in creative writing, it could mean the vocal quality of the language. Texture adds a real depth, richness and sense of dimension to a creative piece.

Thinking points

● There are often valuable associations to be made between texture in different art forms, particularly when it comes to linking up two or more forms, or describing how a piece of art works.

● For example, you might talk about the way that an artist has layered paint to give a three-dimensional effect, or how a composer has added texture to a piece of music through the use of different instrumental sounds.

● Texture has the useful attribute of encouraging the viewer/audience/reader to connect with the piece. It draws all our senses into the equation and we feel more fully engaged with the creative experience.

Tips, ideas and activities

● Get your pupils to create some interactive children's books for the younger children in the school. Show them how they can use texture to encourage young children to use their senses. There are many great touchy-feely books around. (I particularly like the Usborne *That's Not My …* series.)

● Brainstorm words that suggest texture and explore how these might be used in a story, poem or piece of non-fiction writing. (A thesaurus is very useful for this.) Talk about the onomatopoeic qualities of many of these words. You might like to brainstorm under various categories, such as:
  ● 'hard' textures: rough, scrape, scratchy, jagged, bumpy, coarse;
  ● 'soft' textures: smooth, fluffy, squashy, limp, silky, velvety;
  ● 'sound' textures: bang, crash, jingle, swish, thud.

● Explore the different textures that can be made by natural materials. You might ask the children to:
  ● create a collage of texture words, using materials with textures related to the meaning of the vocabulary (for instance, sticking sand onto the word 'rough' or feathers onto the word 'fluffy');
  ● dip into a feely bag and talk about the textures of the different materials they feel;
  ● explore the range of sounds that can be made by the interaction between two or more natural materials (for example, rough bark scraped by a coarse stone).

● Use the textures of various fabrics to inspire some creative work. Your children could:
  ● design and make a costume incorporating lots of different textures;
  ● create a highly textured hand puppet;
  ● sew a variety of materials together to create a blanket of many textures.

You Can... Use movement more creatively

Although movement is often linked with PE (in particular dance) it actually plays a key role in many creative forms. Think of the movement that a painter can achieve with the strokes of a brush, or the sense of motion that we might feel when we listen to some instruments going up and down a scale in a piece of music.

Thinking points

● Some aspects of school require extended periods of concentration, stillness and silence. Giving your pupils plenty of opportunities to be active and to move around is an important counterbalance to this requirement.

● For those children who like to learn in a kinaesthetic way, lessons involving movement offer a chance to build self-confidence and self-esteem.

● There are many interesting links between literacy and movement – the words that we use to describe movement, the way that language can seem to move and pull us along and so on.

● There are also many connections to science in this theme, particularly around the idea of forces.

Tips, ideas and activities

● Get your pupils to create a drawing based around the theme of 'movement', using lines, shapes, different directions, brush strokes and so on.

● Explore different ways of moving by using some drama exercises. Here are some ideas:
  ● Get your pupils to explore adverbs that can describe how we move (for instance, walking limply, running lazily or skipping crazily).
  ● Divide the class into groups and give each group some chairs. Suggest various vehicles (racing car, aeroplane, jeep, motorbike). Ask the children to simulate how they would move when seated in these types of transport.
  ● Give an adjective (smooth, hot, sharp) and ask the children to devise a short piece of dance drama, using this word to inspire their movements.

● Dance notation is a way of documenting and mapping the movements of a piece of dance. Get your pupils to experiment with their own ways of 'writing down' movements, creating their own symbolic language for recording a dance.

● Try this drama activity to encourage creativity and quick thinking around the theme of 'keeping moving':
  ● Divide the class into groups of three or four.
  ● Ask the children to decide on different positions – there should be one for each member of the group. So, a group of four might have: sitting, standing, lying down and crouching.
  ● Set a simple scenario; for instance, breakfast time or getting ready for school.
  ● When you say 'go', the children should begin to improvise.
  ● At all times during the scene, each of them must be in one of these positions; that is, one person sitting, one standing, one lying down and one crouching.
  ● As soon as one person changes position, another must take their place.

You Can... **Create original and imaginative characters**

The best stories are those in which the characters hold our interest. It can be surprisingly hard to create complex and realistic people to put in our stories. The tendency is often to come up with a character who is nice and 'normal', rather than complex and flawed.

Thinking points

● When reading a novel, if we associate strongly with the lead character, this helps us feel engaged with the story and keen to know how things turn out.

● Many of the most interesting characters in literature have some pretty serious flaws, for instance, the classic detective with a very short fuse or a drink problem.

● By studying the way that writers create their characters, we can learn some important lessons about how it is done. Encourage your pupils to read a wide variety of books, preferably in a range of different genres, to see all the different possibilities for characterization and plot.

Tips, ideas and activities

● Look at extracts from stories where a character is described in an interesting way. Talk with your class about what it is that makes these particular characters seem original and engaging.

● A character facing a struggle or an obstacle is far more interesting than someone who has an easy life. The majority of fairy tales are based around a struggle that must be overcome. Help your pupils create their own character obstacles:
  ● First, think of a character (for example, a prince).
  ● Now think of something that this person really wants (for example, to marry a beautiful princess).
  ● Next, come up with a potential obstacle, or series of obstacles. For example, the beautiful princess might be locked up in a tower (as in 'Rapunzel') or in a deep, magical sleep (as in 'Sleeping Beauty').
  ● Now write a story showing how the person overcomes these obstacles.
  ● You can take the same approach for more up-to-date characters. For instance, a boy really wants to play for the school football team, but his family is too poor to buy him some boots, and his main rival for the team is the biggest bully in the school.

● Another way to create interesting characters is to exaggerate certain features. For example:
  ● the loudest hippo in the jungle;
  ● the biggest giant in the world;
  ● the girl whose nose kept growing.

● Similarly, characters with a flaw will be more interesting than those who are perfect in every way. So, a person might:
  ● have a very short temper;
  ● be too nice, so that people take advantage;
  ● have a fault, such as jealousy or greed.

You Can... Develop interesting plots

A good story has a number of key attributes. It will have a clear, developing structure, imaginative dialogue and interesting, engaging characters. Achieving all this can be tricky even for adults; for children, it is a challenging activity.

Thinking points

● There can be a tendency for children to either write about their own lives and experiences, or alternatively to devise stories based on a film or television programme they have seen. While there is nothing essentially wrong with this, it does mean that their stories can lack the imaginative, original element that makes for a really interesting piece of creative writing.

● Analysing the way that other writers plot their stories is a great way to show your pupils the technique, as well as the creativity, inherent in story writing.

Tips, ideas and activities

● Use dialogue as a starting point for developing interesting stories:

- Divide the class into small groups to brainstorm three snippets of dialogue (for instance, 'Get me out of here!', 'It's going to fall!' and 'I can't believe you did that!').
- Get the children to write each line out on a slip of paper, fold it up and put it in a bag.
- Pass the bag around. Each group takes one slip and then uses the line they picked to inspire a storyline.
- Alternatively, do this individually, with each child adding and taking one line.

● Do some detailed analysis of plot structures with your pupils. Use the photocopiable sheet on page 60 ('Story structure') to establish the arc of a storyline:

- Talk about how stories typically develop, build to a climax and end with a resolution.
- Find a short story with a clear narrative arc. You might choose a modern story, a fable or a fairy tale. Something like 'The Three Little Pigs' works well.
- Read the story through with your class. Identify five key points in the story. In 'The Three Little Pigs' these might be: 1. The pigs leave home. 2. The straw house is destroyed. 3. The stick house is destroyed. 4. The brick house stands firm. 5. The wolf ends up in the pot.
- Ask your pupils to draw these images in the five storyboard boxes and put a quote below each one.
- Get them to plot the level of tension at each point in the story, on the graph, above each of the boxes.
- Try this for various stories – in some, the tension might build gradually; in others, the line could stay flat with a sudden climax near the end.

You Can... Create dramatic tension in stories

Dramatic tension is vital for keeping the reader (or audience) engaged with what is happening in a story, whether in a book, film or on the stage. Although it is at its most obvious in action and adventure stories, conflict between characters or within relationships can add dramatic tension and interest to even the simplest of plots.

Thinking points

● Think with your pupils about what tension actually is, both in a personal context and also in stories they have read or watched on television. You might ask the children to feel for the tension that they habitually carry in their bodies.

● Dramatic tension has the effect of keeping us interested in a story. We want to know what happens next, and we will keep reading or watching to find out. This is why chapters in books and episodes in dramas often end with a 'cliff-hanger' moment.

● Dramatic tension also encourages us to feel part of a story. The classic example is a horror film where we want to desperately shout out to a character, 'Don't go into that house/room/spooky forest!' Again, the sense of involvement created is great for keeping us engrossed in the story.

Tips, ideas and activities

● Enclosed spaces create a high level of tension – think of how you feel stepping into a lift with a stranger. Use this idea to help your children develop some dramatically interesting stories – either for a drama session, or as the basis for a creative writing piece. For instance, they could set a story in:
  - a lift that gets stuck between floors;
  - a submarine trapped at the bottom of the sea;
  - a cave where a rock fall has trapped some pot-holers;
  - a spaceship drifting in outer space.

● Use drama to explore how our body language changes when we feel tense. Talk with your class about how this creates a feeling of suspense for an audience. Try this activity:
  - Take your class into an open area, such as a hall or gym.
  - Get the children to stand on their own in a space.
  - Ask them to close their eyes and imagine it is getting dark; they are walking along the street when they realise someone is following them.
  - When you say 'go', they start to move, showing the tension in the way that they use their bodies.
  - Afterwards, talk about the kind of body language and movements that were used.

● A story with a series of escalating problems creates an ever-rising feeling of tension. The film *Jaws* makes use of this effect. Get your pupils to create a storyboard of a situation with a series of problems. For instance, in a story set on a spaceship:
  - a quarrel breaks out among the crew;
  - one of the astronauts gets sick;
  - the engine fails;
  - the ship encounters a strange craft;
  - an alien arrives on-board!

You Can... Use limits to inspire creative writing

It is tempting to believe that, when we are involved in the act of creativity, the artwork (whether painting, story, poem, dance, etc) should just 'flow' out of us. In fact, it is the discipline behind the creative impulse, and the structures within which we work, which help us to create a high-quality finished piece.

Thinking points

● Although it seems counter-intuitive, it is often the case that adding artificial limits to developing a piece of creative writing will actually encourage greater creativity. Having to work within tight limits can help push us into taking more imaginative routes.

● Using plenty of short, limited tasks is a great way to keep your pupils focused and working at their hardest. It also gives you the chance to incorporate plenty of rewards into your lessons.

● The haiku form of poetry is an extreme example of how using a very limited structure can discipline the writer into creating a piece with great clarity, simplicity and beauty.

Tips, ideas and activities

● Here is an activity designed to get your pupils choosing the best vocabulary for a piece of poetry:
   ● Give the class a topic, such as 'cats' or 'the sea'.
   ● Set a time limit (three minutes is about right).
   ● When you say 'go', the children should brainstorm as many words as they can around the topic.
   ● If you like, you might set a challenge to see who can find the highest number of words.
   ● At the end of the time, ask the children to count how many words they have and write this number down.
   ● Next ask them to write down the number that is exactly half this amount.
   ● Now give them another time limit and ask that they cut the original amount down to this number. Encourage them to delete any words that are not particularly interesting, and to keep the 'best' vocabulary.
   ● When this is done, get the children to write these words out on slips of paper. Now ask them to arrange the vocabulary into a word picture or poem.

● Get your children to explore the way that adjectives and adverbs work, and to consider whether a piece of creative writing is 'better' with or without them. Try this activity:
   ● Ask the children to pick a story they have written which contains plenty of adjectives and adverbs. Take a photocopy of the story to work with.
   ● Using a highlighter, get them to go through the story and mark all examples of adjectives and adverbs.
   ● Now get them to rewrite the story, removing all the adjectives and adverbs. These might simply be left out, or they could be replaced with a more detailed description.

You Can... **Take creative approaches to non-fiction**

We might feel that story writing is about creativity, whereas non-fiction writing is about technique and analytical thinking. In fact, the best non-fiction will often have a highly creative element, whether this is to do with form, vocabulary, writing style or imagery.

Thinking points

● Non-fiction is sometimes seen as a bit of a 'poor relation' to fiction. In fact, we are immersed in non-fiction writing in our everyday lives: from the blurb on cereal packets to the scripts for adverts.

● It is tempting to believe that non-fiction writing is always factual, straightforward and honest. Often, though, there is a hidden agenda of some kind. Consequently it is important to have an understanding of the techniques that non-fiction writers might use to persuade, encourage and engage us.

● Encourage your pupils to read a wide range of non-fiction, in lots of different forms. As well as having fictional reading books for the class, offer access to magazines, newspapers, leaflets, brochures and websites as well.

Tips, ideas and activities

● Get your children to analyse and notate some published non-fiction writing, to identify the various techniques that writers use to make their work more creative, persuasive or engaging. For instance, you could:
  ● look at various newspaper reports about the same subject;
  ● ask the children to highlight any emotive words;
  ● examine the way that quotes from 'experts' are used to lend credence to a report;
  ● talk about what the writer wants us to feel about the topic, and how they achieve this.

● Teach your pupils how to 'echo' the topic of a piece of non-fiction writing through the way that they use language. This can be done at different levels, depending on the age and ability of the children. Here are some techniques they could learn to use:
  ● Choosing vocabulary with the appropriate 'tone': a report celebrating the school sports day would use positive, happy sounding language (cheer, delighted, excited) while a report on global warming might use rather doom-laden vocabulary (concerns, fears, uncertain future).
  ● Using lots of questions to engage the readers and make them feel involved: a leaflet about bullying might ask 'What can we do about it?' and 'What can *you* do about it?'
  ● Devising an extended metaphor, appropriate to the topic, to create a sense of connection: a newspaper article about the latest celebrity chef might say he plans to 'spice things up' and that his manner is 'mostly sweet, but sometimes sour'.

● Having a school newspaper or magazine, perhaps published once a term, is a great way to encourage more involvement and creativity in non-fiction forms. If you are willing, you could organise a team of volunteers (pupils and staff) at your school. Alternatively, you might run this as a whole-class project over a half term.

You Can... Get creative with 'What's in the news?'

Topical stories are always a great way of getting your pupils engaged with their learning. Children seem to respond really well to work done in the classroom which has a genuine link to what is happening in the outside world.

Thinking points

● Natural disasters often seem to bring out the best in people, with the public response being one of caring and generosity. Perhaps this is because of the feeling that these events are so random, and that they could so easily happen to us.

● It is interesting to explore how natural events in different parts of the world are given a different level and type of coverage in the media. Talk with your pupils about why this might be.

● While the factual element of geographical news stories is obviously important, taking a creative approach will help your children understand the personal and individual stories behind the news.

Tips, ideas and activities

● Use the floods at Boscastle as the inspiration for looking at how news stories work, and for thinking about the human dimension behind the news. The following websites offer good material for reference:
   ● BBC news report: http://news.bbc.co.uk/1/hi/england/cornwall/3571v44.stm
   ● images of the flood: www.tintagelweb.co.uk/BoscastleFlood.htm
   ● a pamphlet about the flood produced by North Cornwall District Council: www.ncdc.gov.uk/media/adobe/e/s/BoscastleFlood.pdf

● Explore the way that emotive words are used to recreate a sense of the disaster in non-fiction reports. Your pupils might identify aspects such as:
   ● quotes from 'important' visitors to the disaster area (Prince Charles, for example);
   ● language used to create sensory images of the event;
   ● quotes from reliable sources, such as the emergency services and the Environment Agency;
   ● emotive (but often appropriate) vocabulary such as 'deluge', 'destruction' and 'torrential rain';
   ● personal stories that add a human element to the story; for instance, the baby rescued in a rucksack.

● Get your class to recreate and dramatise the event, to help them understand what it might have been like to experience such a natural disaster. Working in groups, the class could:
   ● find ways to recreate the sounds of the flood; for instance, by playing percussive instruments;
   ● create a soundtrack of the voices of the local people – shouts, cries, thought tracking their feelings and so on;
   ● produce a series of freeze-frames to show the progress of the disaster.

● Ask your children to take one image from the websites given and write the story that goes with it.

You Can... Get creative with 'Ancient Greeks'

The Ancient Greeks had a fascinating culture – so much of our modern life can be traced back to their philosophies, ideas and creative works. The fact that they were also powerful fighters and accomplished athletes is of course also very engaging and exciting for children.

Thinking points

● Asking your pupils to 'take on' characters in a history lesson, and to dramatise historical events (both large and small), is a great way of bringing the stories of the past to life.

● Drama is also a really useful approach for getting children to empathise with and understand another culture, time and people. By becoming someone else, and going through what they experienced (even if in a rather superficial way), the children get a taste of another lifestyle.

● There are many links between the study of history and the creative arts, particularly drama. Both deal with people – often colourful characters, and both explore our responses and actions in high pressure situations.

Tips, ideas and activities

● Get your class to do some creative activities and in-role work, based around the two states of Sparta and Athens. First, do some research into what these states were like. The following website is useful as a starting point: http://woodlands-junior.kent.sch.uk/Homework.

● Divide the class into two halves – one half will be the Spartans, the other half the Athenians. Ask both groups to devise five statements about what their city state was like. For instance: *We live in a democracy* (Athens); *Our children learn to be fighters* (Sparta).

● Ask the children to prepare a series of freeze-frames to show what daily life was like in their city state. Each freeze-frame should match up with one of the statements they have chosen. For example, we might see young boys training for the army in Sparta to link with the statement: *Our children learn to be fighters*. They might prepare these freeze-frames as a single large group, or split into smaller groups, allocating one or more to each.

● Now ask the children to 'unfreeze' the scene to show a short piece of action (rather like pausing and then playing a video), then refreeze after about 30 seconds. They could add speaking or sound effects to the action. Watch each of the groups perform in turn.

● Here are some other creative ideas for working with Greek characters:
  - a *Crimewatch* reconstruction of one of the stories (for instance, Artemis shooting Orion);
  - a news report about the Olympians overthrowing the Titans;
  - a collage of Ancient Greek heroes and some modern-day equivalents.

You Can... Get creative with 'Forces in action'

By finding links between science and real world situations, you can show your children how vital scientific understanding is in our everyday lives. The bungee jumping activity below does exactly this – originally designed for an A level physics lesson, it can easily be adapted to suit pupils of various ages.

Thinking points

● Finding answers in science is not just about factual knowledge – in fact, many of the great scientific breakthroughs have come about via creative thinking. The story of Newton's apple is the classic example of this.

● Some scientific skills, such as experimentation and hypothesising, require a high level of creativity. These skills are closely linked to those used in the arts subjects.

● Often, the best ideas (whether scientific or creative) will seem way ahead of their time. The willingness to be bold about our creative thought is a key element in innovation. Unfortunately, the way that our school system is designed will often discourage this kind of innovative, forward-thinking approach.

Tips, ideas and activities

● Take a creative approach to the QCA activity on stretching elastic bands, doing it under the title of 'Bungee-jumping teddies':
  ● Discuss the essential safety elements for a bungee jump. What factors need to be taken into account? (The weight of the jumper and the elasticity and length of bungee rope.) What do bungee jumpers need to know/do/test before a jump?
  ● Do some additional research on the internet. See the British Elastic Rope Sports Association (www.bungeezone. com/orgs/bersa.shtml).
  ● Explain that you are going to bungee jump some teddies/toys. Get the children to bring in some favourites, or borrow some toys from a Key Stage 1 class.
  ● Choose an appropriate location for the bungee jump. This should be a high place in the school with room for the teddies to make their jump; for instance, at the top of a staircase. (Take any safety factors into account.)
  ● Find a way of measuring the distance from the jump point to the ground. Depending on how high it is, they might need to employ creative thinking.
  ● Give the children a variety of pieces of elastic and rope – different lengths, thicknesses, strengths, amounts of elasticity and so on.
  ● Explore what happens to the different pieces of elastic when various weights are added. Record the measurements on a graph.
  ● Find a way of measuring the weight of the teddies without actually testing them on the elastic.
  ● Devise a harness system for attaching the teddies to the rope.
  ● Bungee jump your teddies!

● Explain that some people think that the moon would be a good place to hold extreme sports events, such as skateboarding and mountain bike jumping, due to the rugged terrain and lack of gravity. Brainstorm a list of other activities that you could do on the moon to make use of the lack of gravity. Consider the various advantages and disadvantages of each one.

You Can... Get creative with 'Writing for different audiences'

Although we can make an artwork solely for the personal pleasure of creativity, it is the reaction and response of an audience which in some way validates what we have done. Understanding the role of audience, and choosing the appropriate form, language, presentation and so on is a key skill in developing creativity.

Thinking points

● Many artists work mainly within a particular form, and using a certain style, with a clear understanding of what their audience 'expects', for instance, a painter who creates watercolour landscape pictures or a novelist who writes in the crime genre.

● Although these artists do not necessarily pander to audience expectations, they have a clear sense of what will be pleasing or interesting to the viewer/reader/listener.

● Some artists push at the boundaries, taking little or no account of the potential audience for their work. In fact, the intention or outcome might be to shock and horrify onlookers.

● Creative innovations often come about when the audience's view or response is seen as irrelevant; for instance, Marcel Duchamp's 'readymades' (found objects, such as a urinal, presented as art) or the punk movement in music.

Tips, ideas and activities

● Use the photocopiable sheet on page 61 ('Text effects') as a starting point for some whole-class or group discussions. Talk with your children about:
  - the effects given by the various fonts;
  - what type of audience or form (book, newspaper and so on) each font might best suit;
  - how the 'feel' of the writing changes between upper and lower case;
  - what happens to the effect on the reader when the size of the writing changes;
  - how adding bold, italic, underlining and so on can make the text look different, and the uses these formats might have;
  - the effects that can be created by using coloured text, and how this might relate to different types of audience.

● Try this labelling activity to encourage your pupils to think about the appropriate presentation for different products/audiences:
  - Choose a range of different packaged products, such as dog food, soft drinks, cereals and toys.
  - Remove the labels from cans and bottles, and stick plain paper over the boxed products.
  - Explain to the children that they are going to be working as 'design consultants' to re-brand some products.
  - Discuss each of the products in turn – what is it, who is it for, what will the audience expect? You might look at the 'old style' labels.
  - Use ICT to design new labels for each item, thinking carefully about appropriate fonts and text effects.
  - Note, for some items such as children's foods, the buying 'audience' will be different to the consuming one.

● For an unusual movement-based activity, ask your children to translate different fonts and text effects into a piece of dance. For example, the *Kuenstler Script* font might suggest curling, flowing movements whilst the **Comic Sans MS** font could indicate a simple, clear set of movements.

You Can... Get creative with 'Take a seat'

This art and design topic has some really interesting cross-curricular and multicultural links. Drawing these out during the course of the topic will allow you to incorporate plenty of imaginative activities and creative thinking into your lessons.

Thinking points

● Although seats are very much an everyday piece of furniture, they also have some fascinating symbolic and cultural associations. The 'throne' appears in many cultures, often with carvings or decorations which have great symbolic meaning.

● Our pupils spend a huge amount of time at school sitting in chairs. Unfortunately, many school chairs are not particularly well designed for comfort and posture.

● While we are happy to use carpet time for Key Stage 1 pupils, this is often dispensed with by the start of Key Stage 2. Sitting on the floor with your pupils makes a lovely informal setting for storytelling, drama or discussion work.

Tips, ideas and activities

● Put a row of seats in various locations to inspire some drama around this topic. Set up a line of about five chairs, and ask the children to go straight into an improvisation based in that setting. For instance, your seats might be:
  ● on a tube train or bus;
  ● in a dentist's waiting room;
  ● outside the head teacher's office;
  ● at a football match.

● Bring a variety of different seats into your classroom, for instance, a bar stool, a garden chair, a baby's highchair, etc. Get the children to use these as the basis for a piece of drama or a story.

● Get the children to work together to create a 'throne' for your classroom. Use this as part of your reward system; the child who earns the right to sit in it gets to be king or queen for the day. Spice up this idea further by creating a set of robes, a crown and a sceptre.

● Do some practical experiments to show your pupils how it feels to sit in different ways, and the messages that different seating positions can send. For instance, how would they perceive you if you sat on the floor to teach, on a desk, or on a window ledge?

● Find a broken chair and bring it into class to inspire some creative thinking. Ask your pupils to devise a story to explain how the chair got damaged.

You Can... Get creative with 'Christian religious buildings'

Throughout the ages, people of many different religions have used creativity to demonstrate their faith. One aspect of this is of course the design and construction of beautiful places of worship. The atmosphere within these buildings can give us a sense of mystery and wonder.

Thinking points

● It is interesting to explore the 'feel' and symbolic potential of the various positions we might take up within a church. For instance, kneeling or prostrating yourself features in many different religions and has clear symbolic significance.

● Different faiths use art in very different ways. For instance, Islamic art focuses on glorifying the word of God, particularly through beautiful writing.

● Although religious buildings and symbols vary from faith to faith, it is also interesting to look for connections and links between the art and architecture of different religions.

● One area where many religions share a bond is in the production of beautiful versions of their holy books. You might look at some calligraphy with your class, and talk about why so much effort is focused on the artwork in these texts.

Tips, ideas and activities

● Explore the different images and colours seen in stained glass windows, looking at what they add to Christian religious buildings:
  ● Type 'stained glass windows' into an internet search engine, to find a huge array of pictures to share with your class (copyright permitting).
  ● Talk with the children about the symbolism, meaning and effect of using coloured glass.
  ● Discuss what happens when light shines through a stained glass window – how might this add to the atmosphere within a church?
  ● Get the children to make some stained glass windows of their own, using card and coloured cellophane sheets.

● Get your pupils to build their own church, using the photocopiable sheet on page 62 ('Build a church'). You may wish to enlarge the template onto A3 sheets. Here is what they should do:
  ● Cut out the sections of the building, removing the window shapes to leave a space.
  ● Stick the sections onto card, cutting through the card where the windows will be.
  ● Add coloured cellophane from the inside to the window gaps, to create the effect of stained glass windows. (Your more dextrous children might like to make miniature stained glass windows to go inside.)
  ● Decorate the exterior of the church, colouring the bricks.
  ● Connect the sections together by gluing the tabs and fixing in place.
  ● If possible, get the children to also make an altar and some pews to go inside.
  ● Fix the building onto a piece of stiff card.
  ● Decide on a location for the church, and the kind of surroundings it will sit within.
  ● Create a garden area or cemetery around the church.
  ● Create a sign giving the name of the church and a message for worshippers.

You Can... Get creative with 'Animal magic'

The animal kingdom features a huge diversity of size, colour, shape, movement and so on. It is no wonder, then, that animals have proved to be an inspiration for artists working in various disciplines, and perhaps especially so in music.

Thinking points

● Translating one thing (such as the way that an animal moves) into another form (for example, music, language, art) will help your children learn and understand the art of symbolic representation.

● Many composers, such as Camille Saint-Saëns, have had great success in creating sounds inspired by animals, in a way that brings them to life in our minds. Similarly, many poets have brought animals to life using both the sound and imagery of language.

● As well as sticking to 'real life' animals that actually exist, your pupils can have great fun with creating their own, imaginative creatures. These fantasy animals could then go on to inspire more creative work in literacy lessons.

Tips, ideas and activities

● Try this fun soundtracking activity with your class, to explore how animal sounds can be put together to great effect:
  ● Get the children to lie on the floor in a circle, feet facing out and heads to the middle, so that their ears are almost touching. (With a smaller class, you might do this as one unit, or you could split a large class into two or three groups.)
  ● Give them an animal-related scenario; for instance, 'a rainstorm in the jungle' or 'whales that meet deep in the ocean'.
  ● The children should create a 'soundtrack' using vocal sounds and their bodies. The aim is to start quietly, build up and then gradually fade out, just like a piece of music.
  ● Record some of the soundtracks and let the class listen back to them.

● Get your children to explore fantastical animals, looking at how these can be brought to life using various arts disciplines. You could get the children to:
  ● research some of the imaginative animals created by writers and artists (for instance, the 'wild things' in Maurice Sendak's book, *Where the Wild Things Are* or the creatures in Lewis Carroll's poem, 'Jabberwocky');
  ● create collages of bizarre new creatures using cut out parts of various animals (for instance, an elephant's head on a lion's body, with a parrot's wings);
  ● think about the kind of sounds these bizarre creatures might make, and record some sound effects to go with their collages;
  ● make up some new words to describe how their fantastical creatures move.

● Research the various types of dinosaurs (always a popular topic with children). Explore how dinosaurs of different sizes, shapes, colours and so on might be brought to life using sound, music, drama and movement.

You Can... Get creative with 'Les sports'

The idea that children should be introduced to a foreign language as young as possible is gradually becoming accepted. By using a popular topic such as sport as the basis for your teaching, you should hopefully appeal to all the children in your class, including those who might be less well motivated.

Thinking points

● In some schools, particularly those with a large multicultural population, many of the children will be fluent in two or even more languages. For these children, picking up an additional language will typically be fairly straightforward.

● Other children will live in an area with little cultural diversity, and consequently will have less chance to hear and experience other languages. It is perhaps even more important for these children to get the chance to learn another language at a young age.

● It is all too easy for the British to be lazy about learning a foreign language, because so many people in other parts of the world speak English. However, the ability to communicate in other languages is not only useful for learning about other cultures, it is also a simple matter of politeness.

Tips, ideas and activities

● Ask your pupils to work in pairs or small groups to devise freeze-frames of various sports. Challenge the class to look at these and call out the correct French name. Now do the same with various sporting movements; for instance, 'kick' or 'dive'.

● Try this sports-related activity to encourage your pupils to research and write about life in France, and to learn basic vocabulary and phrases:

- Explain to the class that a famous English footballer is planning a move to a top French team that plays in Paris (for example, Paris St Germain).
- He has asked for information about the country, and to be taught some key French vocabulary (for general daily living and also sports-related words to use in training sessions).
- The children are going to work as 'travel advisors' to research the country and prepare a short booklet or brochure.
- They are also going to give a short lesson in which they will teach the footballer important words and phrases.
- The booklet might include: maps of the area, images of different football moves with related vocabulary, details of the cuisine, information about currency, details for sightseeing, cultural events, etc.
- If possible, ask a member of staff or a willing parent to come into your classroom and play the part of the footballer, so that the children can try out their teaching skills.

● Some children might like to experiment with writing and recording a sports report in French. This could be done by using some TV footage of a sports event with the sound turned down.

You Can... Get creative with 'Sandwich snacks'

Devising recipes and preparing food can be a wonderfully creative activity. The type of ingredients you use, the way that they are combined and the presentation of the final dish all allow for plenty of self-expression and imaginative input.

Thinking points

● Although the daily grind of meal preparation is often mundane, there can be something wonderfully relaxing about cooking, especially when it is done for others.

● Cooking has rightly become ever more popular, particularly since the advent of 'celebrity chefs'. The campaign for better, healthier school meals is one really positive aspect of television cooking.

● Today, the idea that ingredients should be chosen with care, and sourced locally where possible, means that we are ever more careful about and interested in our food.

● Young people can be resistant to change, particularly when it involves eating salads and other healthy foods. Inspiring your children to prepare their own food in an imaginative and creative way should encourage them to eat a more varied diet.

Tips, ideas and activities

● Use some cookery formats from the television to add spice to your sandwich preparation. Here are some possibilities:
   ● Make a children's show in the format of CBBC's *Big Cook Little Cook* aimed at teaching sandwich recipes to younger children. Your pupils could record a show, play it to younger children at the school, and ask for feedback.
   ● Use the *Ready Steady Cook* approach, dividing the class into teams. Each team is given a carrier bag containing ingredients, and they must use these in the most creative way possible. Hold a 'red tomatoes' and 'green peppers' vote at the end to decide who has been the most imaginative.

● Get lots of variety into your sandwich snacks, encouraging your children to use their creative thinking. They might:
   ● use a range of fillings;
   ● try a variety of types of bread;
   ● add various different toppings and garnishes to the finished product;
   ● cut the sandwiches into a range of interesting shapes;
   ● give imaginative names to their sandwich creations.

● Explore with your class where the term 'sandwich' comes from. Challenge your children to come up with a modern name to replace it.

● Get your children to think about their sensory responses to different sandwiches, by smelling and tasting some fillings with a blindfold on.

● Start a discussion on the topic of food hygiene by putting a plastic fly on a sandwich. Talk with the children about what the fly might be doing to their food!

● Ask your pupils to write a recipe for an imaginary sandwich for a character from a favourite story. The more original, imaginative and even disgusting this is, the better!

You Can... Get creative with 'Moving on'

There are many times in our lives when we will have to move on from a well-known situation, to one in which there is much uncertainty. Learning how to cope with such moves and changes, in a positive and confident way, is a key lesson in the process of growing up.

Thinking points

● The period leading up to the move to secondary school will be both an exciting and a worrying time for your pupils. Many urban myths have evolved about what happens when children arrive at secondary school – thankfully, the majority of these are total fiction.

● There has been a big increase in awareness about how the transition can affect children, both emotionally and academically. Thankfully, many schools now have very effective 'links' programmes in place, with specialist staff who can help to ease the stresses and concerns of this time.

● Some children inevitably find change harder to deal with than others. Keep an eye out for any children who are particularly nervous about the move, and give them some extra time and support to help them prepare.

Tips, ideas and activities

● Try this drama activity to look at the various stages involved in 'moving on', and the kind of thoughts and feelings people might experience:
  ○ Ask the children to brainstorm various situations where they have to move on (for instance, moving house from one area to another, moving to secondary school, moving to a new country).
  ○ Divide the class into groups. Each group should choose one scenario from the list you have brainstormed.
  ○ Now ask the children to prepare a series of freeze-frames to show before, during and after the move. In each freeze-frame, one person should say out loud what they are thinking or feeling.

● Use the format of an Oprah Winfrey or Trisha style chat show or similar to explore the issue of friends. You might look at how we make and keep friends, and what to do when friends fall out. Here is how to set up the show:
  ○ Pick a confident child to be 'host', or take on this role yourself.
  ○ Choose several volunteers to be guests on the show. Give these pupils some time to talk about what their 'problem' is going to be (for instance, 'My friend doesn't like me any more' or 'I find it hard to make friends').
  ○ Set up a row of chairs at the front of the room where your guests will sit.
  ○ The rest of the class can play the audience.
  ○ The 'host' interviews the guests and then encourages the audience to ask questions and suggest solutions.

● During Year 6, get your pupils to gather ideas, materials, information, photographs and resources to help them create a year book towards the end of the year. Encourage them to be creative and imaginative with the type of things they include.

What makes a 'good' piece of art?

Art Creative Paint Artistic Draw Design Form White Black Inspire Colour Original Imagine Texture Red Collage Yellow Shade Blue Green Beauty

	Pack 1	Pack 2	Pack 3	Pack 4	Pack 5
1st					
2nd					
3rd					

Different kinds of tasks

Use the ideas here for planning lessons to help you include a variety of tasks.

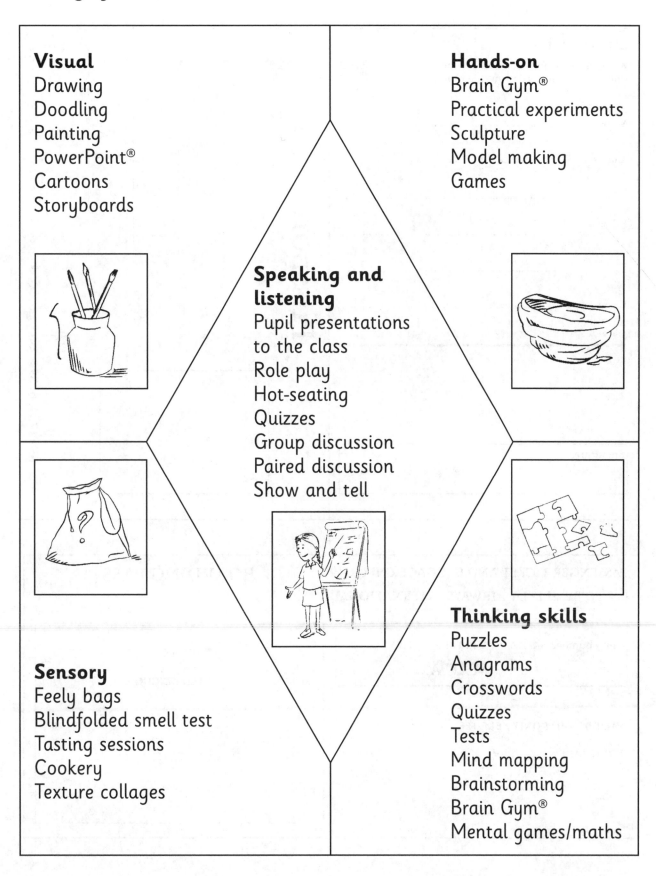

Visual
Drawing
Doodling
Painting
PowerPoint®
Cartoons
Storyboards

Hands-on
Brain Gym®
Practical experiments
Sculpture
Model making
Games

Speaking and listening
Pupil presentations to the class
Role play
Hot-seating
Quizzes
Group discussion
Paired discussion
Show and tell

Sensory
Feely bags
Blindfolded smell test
Tasting sessions
Cookery
Texture collages

Thinking skills
Puzzles
Anagrams
Crosswords
Quizzes
Tests
Mind mapping
Brainstorming
Brain Gym®
Mental games/maths

Passport to the world

Create your own 'passport' and 'airline ticket' to take with you on your trip overseas.

Emergencies

Write the name and address of a friend or family member, who may be contacted in an emergency.

Name: ....

Address: ....

....

....

....

Telephone: ....

Signature:

Passport

Passport No. 123456789

Surname

First name (s)

Date of birth

Place of birth

M/F

A<G BR<123456789<<<<<<<<<<<<<<<<<<<<<<<<<<<<<<<<<<<<

PASSENGER TICKET AND BAGGAGE CHECK
ISSUED BY: SPEEDY AIRWAYS INTERNATIONAL

BOARDING PASS

Flight number: SA1234   1/RETURN   FIRST CLASS

SEAT A...

VALID FLIGHTS ONLY / BKG FEE   £20.00

TOTAL FARE   £110.00

PASSENGER NAME: _____

FROM: UNITED KINGDOM

TO: _____

DATE: _____/_____/_____

TIME: _____

Changing seasons

Story structure

Level of tension

	2.	3.	4.	5.
1.				
Quote:	Quote:	Quote:	Quote:	Quote:

plot

storyline

end

height

tension

middle

structure

excitement

beginning

resolution

climax

Text effects

Headline

HEADLINE

HEADLINE

HEADLINE

HEADLINE

HEADLINE

Small

Medium

Large

Huge

Plain

Bold

Italic

Kuenstler Script

Comic Sans MS

Haettenschweiler

Times New Roman

Build a church

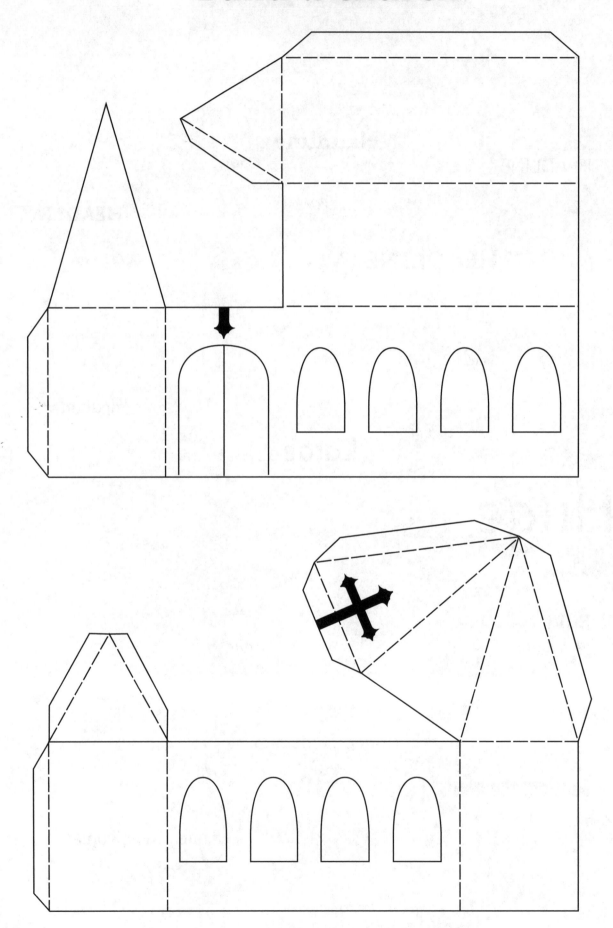

Index

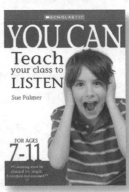